SpringerBriefs in Education

More information about this series at http://www.springer.com/series/8914

DeAnna M. Laverick

Mentoring Processes in Higher Education

Springer

DeAnna M. Laverick
Department of Professional Studies
in Education
Indiana University of Pennsylvania
Indiana, PA
USA

ISSN 2211-1921 ISSN 2211-193X (electronic)
SpringerBriefs in Education
ISBN 978-3-319-39215-8 ISBN 978-3-319-39217-2 (eBook)
DOI 10.1007/978-3-319-39217-2

Library of Congress Control Number: 2016941321

Printed on acid-free paper

This Springer imprint is published by Springer Nature
The registered company is Springer International Publishing AG Switzerland

This book is first dedicated to God and my family. To my husband, Randy, thank you for always encouraging me and believing in me. To my children, Braden and Alaina, cherish the mentoring relationships that you have throughout your life. Whether they take place in academics, athletics, or in personal relationships, appreciate the role that your mentors have played and give back by becoming mentors and positive role models throughout your lives. To my mom and dad, you were my first mentors. Thank you for all that you have done to shape and form me into being the person and mentor that I am today.

This book is also dedicated to the special mentors in my life: Dr. Donald McFeely, Mrs. Janet Kauffman, Mrs. Cheryl Caroff, Mrs. Carol Marcenzo, Dr. Mary Jalongo, Dr. Robert Millward, Dr. Anne Creany, Dr. Susan Fello, Dr. Kelli Paquette, Dr. Valeri Helterbran, Dr. Sue Rieg, and Ms. Pamela Sugg. Each one of you has exerted a positive influence on my life and has taught me so much. I appreciate the time and expertise that you have shared in your own special way.

Acknowledgments

I would like to first thank Dr. Mary Renck Jalongo for her suggestions, ideas, and feedback on this publication. Next, I would like to thank the following individuals for their contribution: Ms. Tenesha Ali; Dr. George Bieger; Ms. Abby Bono; Ms. Megan Carney, Coach William Graham, and the IUP softball team; Mrs. Melissa Casses; Ms. Kaitlyn Colbert; Ms. Courtney Connell; Ms. Emily Deyarmin; Ms. Cassandra Fay; Dr. Thomas Frantz; Ms. Kris Glosser; Mr. Willam Hamilton; Dr. Kelly Heider; Dr. Valeri Helterbran; Ms. Ying Jiang; Dr. Shirley Johnson; Dr. Ali Kappel; Ms. Alaina Laverick; Mr. Randall Laverick; Ms. Danielle Malicky; Dr. Joseph Marcoline; Ms. Diane McCoy; Ms. Hannah Mercer; Dr. Joann Migyanka; Ms. Kimberly Mohney; Ms. Nichol Murray; Ms. Laura Nientimp; Mr. Michael Pampena; Dr. Kelli Paquette; Ms. Alexis Potts; Dr. Sue Rieg; Ms. Ashley Rush; Dr. Susan Sibert; Dr. Meghan Twiest; Mr. William VanEmburg; and Dr. Huachuan Wen. Finally, I would like to thank my graduate assistant, Ms. Nichol Murray, for her assistance with research and manuscript preparation.

Contents

About the Author

DeAnna M. Laverick D.Ed. is Professor and Assistant Chairperson in the Department of Professional Studies in Education Department at Indiana University of Pennsylvania, where she teaches courses in the Early Childhood/Special Education, M.Ed. in Literacy, and Master's in Education programs. Dr. Laverick also chairs and serves on dissertation committees in the D.Ed. in Curriculum and Instruction and D.Ed. in Administration and Leadership Studies programs. Prior to becoming a tenure-track faculty member in 2007, Dr. Laverick was an elementary school teacher and a reading specialist. This experience informs her research-based teaching practice as she instructs teacher education candidates. Her teaching philosophy centers on modeling effective strategies and pedagogy for her students. In 2015, Dr. Laverick was honored with the University Senate Distinguished Faculty Award for Teaching.

Dr. Laverick's research interests are in the areas of early literacy, children's literature, and creative experiences for children. Dr. Laverick co-edited with Dr. Mary Jalongo *Transitions to Early Care and Education: International Perspectives on Making Schools Ready for Young Children,* which is the fourth volume in the *Educating the Young Child: Advances in Theory and Research, Implications for Practice* series. Most recently, Dr. Laverick published the book chapter, "Teaching with Technology and Interactive Media to Promote Creativity and Arts-based Learning in Young Children" in *Young Children and Families in the Information Age,* which was co-edited by Dr. Kelly Heider and Dr. Mary Jalongo. Additionally, Dr. Laverick has recently published in *Journal of Technology and Teacher Education, Reading Improvement, Pennsylvania Reads*, and *Teaching Artist Journal*. Dr. Laverick has made several international, regional, and national conference presentations. She serves as a reviewer for professional journals.

Along with Dr. Joann Migyanka, Dr. Laverick co-advises the Beta Gamma Chapter of Kappa Delta Pi, which is the International Honor Society in Education. She actively serves on university-wide, college-wide, and departmental committees, including the University Wide Graduate Committee and Association for Pennsylvania State College and University Faculties' Scholarship Committee.

Additionally, Dr. Laverick chaired the Mentoring Committee in her department and currently chairs the department's Literacy Committee. Dr. Laverick is the coordinator of the M.Ed. in Literacy/Reading Specialist program and Director of the Literacy Center at Indiana University of Pennsylvania.

Chapter 1
The Mentoring Process

Abstract This chapter provides an overview of the mentoring process, beginning with a theoretical background and research base. The theoretical background and research base establish a rationale for mentoring in higher education. The chapter then shares different mentoring relationships that exist in higher education. The stakeholders in mentoring relationships are described, including faculty, students, and professional colleagues. Characteristics of positive mentors are identified, which serve to provide qualities that potential mentors could develop in order to serve their protégés well. Examples of effective mentoring models and programs are discussed, along with the benefits of mentoring. This chapter serves as an overview for the book, before each chapter provides detailed information on specific mentoring topics.

Keywords Mentors · Mentoring · Mentoring relationships · Theories of mentoring · Mentoring benefits · Characteristics of mentors

1.1 Introduction

When the word "mentor" is mentioned, several connotations come to mind: gifted teacher, trusted guide, inspiration, support system, and role model. Bozeman and Feeney (2007) defined mentoring as "a transmission of knowledge, social capital, and psychosocial support that is related to work" (p. 733). While Jonson (2002) described mentoring as complex and requiring "the skills of a teacher, counselor, friend, role model, guide, sponsor, coach, resource, and colleague" (p. 9), Lea's (2011) view is somewhat different. Lea posited that mentoring differs from "teaching, coaching, counseling, supporting, and protecting" because a "lasting transformational impact" is made in the participants (p. 259). The idea that mentoring may be distinguished from other types of academic relationships was also shared by Zeind et al. (2005) who stated that the two elements that make mentoring unique are the "reciprocity between the mentor and the protégé, and the achievement of an identity transformation by each party" (p. 1). Furthermore, Lea noted

D.M. Laverick, *Mentoring Processes in Higher Education*,
SpringerBriefs in Education, DOI 10.1007/978-3-319-39217-2_1

that mentoring is "significant for its capacity to influence beyond what each isolated role can provide" (p. 259). Lea advised that "mentoring needs to shed the usual assumption of cultural deficit found in the mentees. Roles such as counselor, coach, trainer or supporter superimpose an asymmetrical positionality of power upon the mentee and the mentor" (p. 261).

In higher education, the role of the mentor is critical. As one faculty member described, the role of the mentor is to keep the protégé on the right path to success; their success is the faculty member's goal (Helterbran, personal communication, 2014). The mentor, whether a faculty member or student, is key in helping the protégé transition, adjust, and thrive in this environment. Mentoring in higher education is important "because it raises student achievement, lowers attrition, reduces stress, and makes it more likely that students will be satisfied with the career choices they have made" (Heider, personal communication, 2014).

Mentoring is a process and should be viewed through a developmental perspective (Rodriguez 1995). Mentoring may be thought of as a circular process that begins with a strong mentor who teaches, supports, and inspires the protégé in a cycle of learning that eventually results in the protégé becoming the mentor. Nakamura et al. (2009) stated, "Good mentoring equips new professionals to do good work and provide good mentoring to the next generation as well" (p. 234). These researchers found that "some good mentoring practices tend to be inherited" (p. 234). This cycle has been referred to as a "circle of care" in which the protégé eventually repays the support that was given by helping others by giving them care and support (Sibert, personal communication, 2014). A study conducted by McMahon and Piro (2013) found that preservice teachers who were mentored during a field experience sought to become mentors themselves in the future. This idea is evident in one faculty member's belief about mentoring:

> Education is a caring profession. Mentoring is the right thing to do. Each of us got where we are today based in part on the help and caring of others along the way. Paying it forward is the gold standard of being a good educator. (Helterbran, personal communication, 2014)

There are many types of mentoring situations in higher education that occur within and among faculty, students, and professional colleagues, who are the stakeholders in the mentoring relationship. A review of literature conducted by Lumpkin (2011) identified the following types of mentoring approaches: (1) formal or classic mentoring; (2) informal mentoring; (3) peer mentoring; (4) group, networking, and consortia mentoring; (5) intra-departmental mentoring; (6) inter-department mentoring; and (7) research mentoring.

Daloz (1999) described the role of a mentor as being a guide, a map in a sense, who transmits wisdom by leading the protégé on a journey. He explained,

> Mentors can appear throughout our lives, whenever we encounter a new transition … but mentors are more than simply isolated individuals who enter our lives, intervene, and depart. Rather, they are creations that emerge out of particular demands our lives make on us. When they do their work well, they help us see not only the tasks before us but also the broader context that gives those tasks meaning. (pp. 204–205)

Thinking of mentorship in this way underscores the importance of mentoring in higher education. Bozeman and Feeney (2007) viewed "formal mentoring programs as sowing the seeds of relationships, many of which flower into useful and productive mentor relationships" (p. 733). While the roles of the mentor and the protégé are often prearranged (Lea 2011), considering the best matches for pairing mentors and protégés deserves careful consideration in order to promote positive relationships. Research has shown that "matching mentors and mentees and the skills and attitudes mentors bring to the relationship are crucial issues" (Thurston et al. 2009, p. 404). The study conducted by Thurston et al. found that matching mentors and protégés was very important, with one protégé explaining that having similar professional dispositions was key. Mentors must demonstrate commitment to their protégés and mutually determined needs and expectations should be outlined at the outset of the relationship in order to avoid protégés working with "pseudo mentors" (Collins et al. 2009). In other words, Collins and colleagues explained that pseudo mentors are more focused on their own needs, may not follow through with providing assistance, and do not commit the time that their protégés need.

Rowley (2006) outlined four phases of a mentoring relationship: (1) Initiation, which consists of the introduction and orientation processes and during which the mentors and protégés meet for the first time; (2) Exploration, which is comprised of self-disclosure and acceptance processes and during which the mentors and protégés learn about each other; (3) Collaboration, which includes the processes of sharing and building trust; and (4) Consolidation, in which the processes of respecting and appreciating lead to a deeper appreciation of one another (p. 24).

It is evident that the various definitions and key aspects of mentoring underscore the importance and complexity of developing positive mentoring relationships. The focus of this chapter will now turn toward an overview of the theoretical background and research base on mentoring. The chapter will then share different mentoring relationships that exist in higher education. The stakeholders in mentoring relationships are described, along with the characteristics that positive mentors exhibit. Examples of effective mentoring models and programs are discussed, along with the benefits of mentoring. Informal questionnaire data gathered from colleagues and students are woven throughout *Mentoring Processes in Higher Education*. The author acknowledges the use of informally gathered data as a limitation but also believes that these data are valuable in providing authentic examples to realistically illustrate key points.

1.2 Theoretical Background

This manuscript views the foundation for mentoring in higher education through theories of expertise (Berliner 1994; Chase and Simon 1973; Chi et al. 1988; Ericsson and Smith 1991; Holyoak 1991), human and social capital theories (Bourdieu 1986; Coleman 1990), and the relationship of these theories to adult learning (Alfred 2009).

1.2.1 Theories of Expertise

Expertise refers to "the psychological mechanisms underlying the superior achievement of an expert and the social forces that designate the status of being an expert" (Ericsson and Hoffman 2003, p. 765). Furthermore, expert performance is defined by Ericsson and Hoffman as "the result of skill acquired with gradual improvements of performance during extended experience in a domain" (p. 765). Five developmental stages of becoming an expert have been posed by Dreyfus and Dreyfus (1986) and are referred to as novice, advanced beginner, competent, proficient, and expert. While Chi et al. (1988) noted that ordinary people appear to have the potential for developing expertise, Dreyfus and Dreyfus (1986) explained that not all attain an expert level of skills. Sternberg (1998) posed a theory of developmental expertise that blended the constructs of abilities and expertise. Sternberg (2001) viewed the two constructs as being intertwined and defined expertise as "the ongoing process of the acquisition and consolidation of a set of skills needed for a high level of mastery in one or more domains of life performance" (p. 160).

Teachers who have demonstrated expertise have been described as "superb mentors and role models" (Laverick 2007, p. 248). Expertise should be shared by mentors and developed in their protégés. For example, Larkin (1979) suggested teaching the processes used by experts directly to the students. This notion underscores the importance of mentorship and its role in developing expertise in others. Sternberg (2001) stated, "The main constraint in achieving expertise is not some fixed prior level of capacity, but purposeful engagement involving direct instruction, active participation, role model, and reward" (p. 162). It follows, therefore, that mentors may help develop expertise when they act upon the components of purposeful engagement as described by Sternberg. These ideas are seen in the example shared by a doctoral candidate who described one of her mentors:

> … has been a mentor for most of my life and the opportunity to simply watch her progress through her own doctoral studies and excel has given me the glimpse that great things are possible. The constant and selfless support from a relational standpoint have given me the most benefit to date–the ability to be connected and know that people truly do care about watching others achieve their own greatness–is mentorship in my eyes.

With regard to the role that coaching plays in mentoring, research has shown that good coaching is the second most important variable in development of expertise (Berliner, 2004; Starkes et al. 1996). Laverick's (2005) study of teachers who have demonstrated expertise in teaching early literacy act as mentors and have an impact on supporting new teachers and candidates earning certification by the National Board for Professional Teaching Standards. When these expert teachers were candidates themselves, they had support from colleagues, administrators, families, and other teachers with National Board Certification. These teachers were coached and in turn, act as coaches as they mentor others.

1.2.2 Human and Social Capital Theories

Coleman's (1990) description of physical, human, and social capital informs mentoring processes, relationships, and outcomes. Coleman explained,

> Just as physical capital is created by making changes in materials so as to form tools that facilitate production, human capital is created by changing persons so as to give them skills and capabilities that make them able to act in new ways. Social capital, in turn, is created when the relations among persons change in ways that facilitate action. Physical capital is wholly tangible, being embodied in observable material form; human capital is less tangible, being embodied in the skills and knowledge acquired by an individual; social capital is even less tangible, for it is embodied in the *relations* among people. Physical capital and human capital facilitate productive activity, and social capital does so as well. (p. 304)

When a new person enters a group, whether as a new faculty member, new undergraduate or graduate student, new student teacher or athlete, membership in this group entails socialization and mentoring by someone experienced in the workings of this group. Mentoring helps protégés achieve a sense of belonging (Murray, personal communication, 2014). Mentoring helps protégés learn the culture of an institution and assists with socialization (Zeind et al. 2005). Mentoring is also viewed as a way to combat the challenges associated with socialization (Schrodt et al. 2003). This socialization process may be thought of as means for building social capital. Social capital is defined by Bourdieu (1986) as:

> The aggregate of the actual or potential resources which are linked to possession of a durable network of more or less institutionalized relationships of mutual acquaintance and recognition—or in other words, to membership in a group—which provides each of its members with the backing of the collectively-owned capital, a 'credential' which entitles them to credit, in the various senses of the word. (p. 248)

Johnson (2007) stated, "Well-mentored protégés are introduced to significant people in both the local university community and the broader profession. Compared to nonmentored peers, they report greater organizational influence, more immediate access to important power-holders, and greater allocation of resources" (p. 9). Without mentorship, one may feel isolated and lack the means for developing a strong professional network (Murray, personal communication, 2014). This position is echoed by Alfred (2009) who explained that exclusion and inclusion of individuals in organizations may be influenced by members of social capital networks. It follows, therefore, that strong mentors help protégés gain entry into the networks that will help them be successful in their careers. According to Lea (2011), "The historical value of mentorship builds social, political and intellectual capitals of networks. It resembles transmission of cultural knowledge in the anthropological lineage" (p. 266). "The mentor can also assist the protégés by making explicit what is implicit within an institution" (Zeind et al. 2005, p. 11).

Lumpkin's (2011) review of the literature identified socialization into the academic culture and facilitation of networking as being outcomes of mentoring. These outcomes build human and social capital. Ultimately, according to Lumpkin, through "socialization, support, and networking, protégés are positioned for greater job performance and tend to enjoy higher levels of satisfaction in their work" (p. 364). Feeling connected to others has been a commonly expressed need of new faculty (Searby and Collins 2010) and effective mentoring can help address this need.

"Successful mentoring requires an open, honest, and collaborative relationship between mentor and mentee—a relationship that develops over time" (Thurston et al. 2009, p. 405). Depending on the needs of the protégé and what is offered by the mentor (e.g., wisdom, advice, demonstration of a skill), the flow of the mentoring relationship may ebb over time. Coleman (1990) explained, "Like human capital and physical capital, social capital depreciates if it is not renewed. Social relationships die out if not maintained; expectations and obligations wither over time; and norms depend on regular communication" (p. 321).

1.2.3 *Influence on Adult Learning*

Two approaches to mentoring have been described as aligning with constructivist and behaviourist learning theory (Richter et al. 2013). Richter and colleagues stated that descriptions of constructivist and transmission-oriented (i.e., behaviorist) "mentoring illustrate two different forms of instructional support because the primary goal of mentoring is to foster professional knowledge and skills" (p. 168). They continued, "Emotional support and role modeling of mentors is not explicitly included in both models. Therefore, both approaches characterize only one part of all the functions mentors exercise" (p. 168). Zachary (2000) proposed a learner-centered approach to mentoring in which the protégé shares responsibility for "the learning setting, priorities, learning, and resources, and becomes increasingly self-directed" (p. 3). This model of mentoring helps meet the unique needs of the protégé because of the personal investment made by the protégé in achieving the learning outcomes. According to Zachary, conscious reflection helps adults learn and retain knowledge. She stated:

> Regular mentoring reflection has the following benefits:
>
> - Clarifies thinking
> - Captures the richness of learning experiences
> - Helps to sort out the mentor's feelings about what is occurring
> - Provides a written log with specific details and information
> - Promotes systematic and intentional reflections (pp. 53–54)

Cohen and Galbraith (1995) described mentoring as:

> A one-to-one process of guided developmental learning based on the premise that the participants will have reasonably frequent contact and sufficient interactive time together. Mentors contribute their knowledge, proficiency, and experience to assist mentees who are working toward the achievement of their own objectives. As the relationship evolves, mentees usually interpret the collaborative learning experience with and from their mentors as increasingly important to them. (p. 5)

1.3 Mentoring Relationships

The mentor-protégé relationship is not just one-sided but rather it is a reciprocal process that holds benefits for both the mentor and protégé. Ghosh's (2013) review of the literature on mentoring in the fields of education and business found similarities in that both fields viewed mentoring as being multidimensional, having reciprocity in the mentoring relationship, which manifests over time, and the situation of the mentoring relationship within a professional context that focuses on the professional growth of the protégé. While mutual benefits are derived from mentoring, the reward for mentors is found in the success of the protégé (Helterbran, personal communication, 2014), who elaborated by describing the contribution to the success of others through mentoring as being a joyful experience. In her role as a mentor, Johnson admitted, "I need them as much as they might think they need me. I am looking for personal and professional growth and feel that I can acquire that as we interact with each other" (personal communication, 2014). From a student's perspective, the mentor should be "truly invested in the students they will be mentoring" (Nientimp, personal communication, 2014).

In positive mentor-protégé relationships, mutual trust exists and both parties learn from one another, whereby each brings to the relationship new ideas to share. This relationship forms the basis for reflection, a transaction of ideas, and ultimately growth in knowledge and skills. This growth advances the institution and field due to the positive and collaborative environment, where all stakeholders thrive and are valued for their contributions. According to Schulz (1995), the mentoring relationship becomes co-creative as the partners address similar tasks. Paquette elaborated that learning takes place as a mentor and a protégé; plus, mentors are aware that they are role models and therefore do the best that they can each day (personal communication, 2014). Murray shared that mentoring provides an opportunity for collaboration between mentor and protégé and an opportunity for both to gain knowledge from each other (personal communication, 2014). Positive mentoring relationships should be developed in higher education by regular contact, support, and patience (Bono, personal communication, 2014).

Daloz (1999) described the primary task of the mentor as engendering trust, meaning that the mentor's agenda is suspended in order to understand the student's world. Johnson shared that "developing a level of trust and respect for where the mentee is and what they feel they need is key in the relationship" (personal communication, 2014)

According to Zachary (2000), there is a cycle that consists of four phases that occur in every mentoring relationship:

- Preparing: Mentors explore their motivation for their role, assess their mentoring skills, and identify their learning needs.
- Negotiating: The mentor and mentee agree on the learning goals and define the content and process of the relationship.

- Enabling: The implementation phase in which most of the contact takes place; the mentee's growth and development are nurtured.
- Closing: The partners evaluate, acknowledge, and celebrate achievement of the learning outcomes. (pp. 50–52)

Individual needs should be considered and addressed in each mentoring relationship. The unique mentoring needs of women in higher education should be addressed through mentoring. A student-athlete shared her beliefs about mentoring:

> I believe that everyone is unique in his or her own way. However, I do believe that some women share the same unique mentoring needs. Women have a desire to strive to succeed on their own and with today's generation, that is becoming more and more evident. In order for women to succeed on their own, they need a little help along the way. They need someone whom they look up to and can rely on for continuous support. Women need a mentor who will guide them until they can do it on their own. For example, Hillary Clinton, wife to President Bill Clinton, has achieved many professions of her own over the years with some guidance from her husband, such as, politician, lawyer, and a diplomat. Today, she has become a role model and mentor for thousands of woman around the world. Just like most men, women also have that competitive ego to want to be the best. (Carney, personal communication, 2014)

1.4 Characteristics of Great Mentors

Being a great mentor carries enormous responsibility. When one considers all of the things that mentors do, the role of the mentor cannot be underestimated. Ghosh (2013) identified the following 10 mentoring functions as derived from a review of the literature on mentoring in education: "(a) encouraging reflection; (b) coaching; (c) counseling; (d) assessing; (e) role modeling; (f) being a colleague/fellow learner; (g) parenting; (h) mediating; (i) making friend [*sic*]; and (j) teaching" (p. 156). Ghosh identified encouraging reflective thought, assessing, and teaching as the most challenging functions.

There are many attributes that good mentors share. According to Helterbran, the best mentors don't consider what they are doing as mentoring but rather just part of being a quality, caring educator, which is a natural extension for which they seek no credit or reward (personal communication, 2014). It is important that protégés know about the mentoring support system that is place so that they can access this resource. Additionally, mentors should convey a genuine willingness to assist their protégés so that protégés do not think that they are imposing upon the mentor's time. Daloz (1999) explained that "effective mentors add value and moral content to the relationship" (p. 244).

From a student's perspective, "mentors should create a stress-free, warm environment" (Nientimp, personal communication, 2014). Additionally, a graduate student believed that the most important influence on the efficacy of the mentoring relationship may be the availability and readiness of the mentor in terms of frequent consultation and giving constructive feedback (Wen, personal communication, 2014). A former undergraduate eloquently shared:

> If I did not have my mentors, I would have been lost in a sea of jumbled information. I have to credit my mentors for helping me to graduate. I feel that without them, this process wouldn't have been as smooth. (Malicky, personal communication, 2014)

Zachary (2000) described the learning environment as a "dynamic climate in which learning takes place. It encompasses a varying combination of elements that can include the behavior and attitude of both mentor and mentee, the physical setting, resources and opportunity" (p 120). A study conducted by Schrodt et al. (2003) found:

> New faculty who are mentored feel more connected to their work environments than their non-mentored peers. Protégés also claim to have a greater sense of ownership of their departments, and to receive information about tenure and promotion, research, teaching, and service expectations with greater frequency than non-mentored faculty members. Overall the results indicate that the benefits of mentoring are reciprocal and benefit the institution as well as the protégé. (p. 26)

Schrodt et al. found that protégés' sense of ownership was related to the following five mentoring behaviors: research assistance, protection, collegiality, promotion, and friendship.

Within the working and learning environment, there are characteristics that are valued by protégés such as "respect, honesty, time to devote to being a mentor, encouraging attitude in concert with constructive criticism, high expectations, and knowledge of how to live a balanced life" (Thurston et al. 2009, p. 412). Schrodt et al. (2003) found four themes emerge as descriptors of mentors by their protégés: (1) through family relationships; (2) as a friend; (3) through formal relationships; and (4) in the way that mentors facilitated the growth of their protégés. Table 1.1 presents a description of the characteristics of good mentors, as shared by faculty, graduate students, and undergraduate students.

It is important for mentors to be professional and friendly, according to Malicky, who elaborated, "All of my mentors were extremely kind, welcoming, and helpful. You could tell that they were there to help and wanted the best for you. It is important for the student to feel cared for" (personal communication, 2014).

1.5 Benefits of Mentoring

There are numerous benefits of mentoring, such as personal satisfaction, partnerships, and working for the greater good (Ford, pseudonym, personal communication, 2014). Schulz (1995) described many benefits of mentoring, with the most important benefit as one to society. She elaborated that mentoring is a "win-win situation… It maximizes the human capacity to form attachments and blends with many theories of how adults develop and change through life" (p. 64). Beyond the basic benefit of mentoring, increasing a protégé's knowledge, friendship may also occur (Bono, personal communication, 2014). Ultimately, mentors may help protégés secure jobs in their field.

Table 1.1 Characteristics of good mentors

Characteristics
Demonstrates care and empathy for the protégé
Is knowledgeable and experienced in his or her field; demonstrates wisdom and common sense
Is a good listener and answers questions
Takes a personal interest, including providing advice beyond job responsibilities (e.g., advice on balancing work and personal life); desires to assist and help in any way they can; is generous in sharing ideas and suggestions; puts his or her own ego aside and puts the protégé's best interest at heart
Demonstrates enthusiasm related to education, and is positive
Supports ideas and makes suggestions; values the opinions and initiatives of the protégé; guides the protégé away from counterproductive roles and projects
Is kind, approachable, friendly, and helpful
Provides quality, specific, and direct advice, guidance, and constructive feedback
Is ethical, trustworthy, respected by colleagues, and practices confidentiality
Is available and shares time
Is calm and patient
Encourages and supports
Loves one's job and is encouraging
Motivates others and sets a good example by being a good role model in word and deed
Develops a rapport with the protégé; is collaborative
Helps the protégé problem-solve; is a problem solver
Allows the protégé to observe what the mentor does and how it is done
Finds fulfillment in others achieving their own greatness; genuine (e.g., truly wants to help rather than focus on own agenda)
Sets personal/professional goals–is always growing as an active learner and professional; values ongoing learning and growth in the field
Provides factual information and makes referrals to others who may help
Anticipates a need; is aware of the protégé's level of experience when offering advice and suggestions
Is honest
Builds a relationship based on trust
Shares similar interests with the protégé
Has a willingness to share skills, knowledge, and expertise
Is observant
Has a sense of wanting to give back
Shares resources
Is organized
Provides a neutral person
Is a professional coach
Accepts diverse people and perspectives
Celebrates the protégé's successes
Makes eye contact

Note The characteristics cited in the table are attributed to personal communication with the following sources: Bono, Carney, Casses, Deyarmin, Ford, Heider, Helterbran, Jiang, Johnson, Layton, Malicky, Marcoline, Murray, Nientimp, Paquette, Rieg, Sibert, and Wen

A ten-year mentoring program housed in the College of Education at Kansas State University was described according to the perspectives of administrators, mentors, and protégés (Thurston et al. 2009). Thurston and colleagues noted benefits of mentoring programs in universities, which include: "a stronger presence in research and funding and scholarship, a more dynamic teaching cadre, and an academic team interested in learning, contributing, and growing" (p. 414). These researchers described mentoring relationships as having "a potential transformative power in higher education" and elaborated:

> Mentoring programs in higher education are being developed to advance a diverse faculty, promote supportive academic environments, and recruit and retain outstanding faculty. Effective mentoring programs can assist new professors by coaching them in the formal and informal aspects of the academic culture, helping them develop networks for collaboration, and helping them understand and meet the expectations for promotion and tenure. There are often added benefits for those who mentor, such as renewed interest in the field and the altruistic nature of mentoring. (p. 401)

In addition to characterizing mentoring as being transformative, Lea (2011) described its nature as being constructive and reflexive. Some of the benefits of being mentored and serving as a mentor were described by a faculty member:

> Not only have I made lasting friendships, I've become a successful higher education professional and have seen many of my mentees prosper and grow as professional educators and school administrators. I believe I have learned from my mentees as much, if not more, than they taught me. I have learned different teaching strategies from observing my mentees, read more educational literature by researchers whom I was unfamiliar with, and became more engaged with urban education and PDS partnerships. (Rieg, personal communication, 2014)

This belief illustrates the mutual benefits of mentoring, which include the intrinsic reward of encouraging and guiding protégés (Lumpkin 2011; Zeind et al. 2005). Furthermore, the benefits described by Rieg illustrated the shared environment mentioned by Ortlieb et al. (2010) in which "resources, suggestions, information, and friendship thrived" (p. 109). Ortlieb et al. advised that this shared environment promoted teamwork as opposed to competition that fostered self-attainment.

A doctoral candidate offered her perspective on the benefits of being mentored. "The benefits to having had mentors thus far have been to recognize my ability to achieve and find my own self-confidence. I also think that mentors also are able to find fulfillment in watching their seeds grow" (Casses, personal communication, 2014). This sentiment is echoed in Johnson's belief that one of the benefits of mentoring is HOPE–Helping Other People Excel, which is a way of paying it forward that they will extend a hand to someone else (personal communication, 2014). Similarly, a former undergraduate student explained that "the mentor serves as a source of information and comfort. I used my mentors in answering questions but also to make sure that I was on track and at the top of my game" (Malicky, personal communication, 2014).

Retention is a positive outcome of quality mentoring programs. Mentoring helps retain students, faculty, and administrators by providing supportive frameworks for high quality experiences for students who may be unfamiliar with how to navigate the path to a degree (Johnson, personal communication, 2014). She further explained that mentoring "provides new faculty with the expectations and guidelines to enhance their teaching, scholarship, and service opportunities."

The benefits of mentoring are similar to those of teaching according to a student who explained:

> I feel that a benefit of mentoring involves the joy of being able to help a person learn so that soon they would be able to master the skills they need to succeed. Being a mentor to someone can provoke a chain reaction in that particular person being mentored to want to mentor someone else. (Carney, personal communication, 2014)

Heider (personal communication, 2014) shared that the benefits that a faculty member receives as a result of mentoring include:

- They have a feeling of satisfaction after helping their protégés achieve their goals and, in turn, giving back to their profession.
- They build their leadership and management skills.
- They receive respect and admiration from their protégés and others around them who recognize the time and energy they are devoting to the mentorship.
- They gain new insights and different perspectives from their protégés.

She elaborated by stating that protégés benefit because:

- They get an insider's view of the profession.
- They have someone to go to for advice.
- They have someone to bounce ideas off of.
- They have someone who's "on their side."
- They have someone who will hold them accountable and provide them with constructive criticism.
- They have someone who will "open doors" for them.
- They learn what is needed to be successful and grow in their profession.
- They build their leadership and management skills.
- They increase the capacity to turn theory into practice.

With regard to the leadership skills that are developed as a result of mentoring, Tony Dungy (2010) explained the concept of mentor leaders, who are leaders and also the select few who are mentors. He stated, "Raising up leaders is the truly selfless goal of every mentor leader, the culmination of focusing on others" (p. 188). This goal is important because, as he shared, mentors are building a future generation of leaders. Feldman et al. (2010) found that faculty who were mentored "were more likely to be satisfied with the distribution of their work and had higher self-efficacy than those who were not mentored" (p. 5).

References

Alfred, M. V. (2009). Social capital theory: Implications for women's networking and learning. *New Directions for Adult & Continuing Education, 122*, 3–12.

Berliner, D. C. (1994). Expertise: The wonder of exemplary performances. In J. N. Mangieri & C. C. Block (Eds.), *Creating powerful thinkers in teachers and students* (pp. 161–186). Orlando, FL: Holt, Rinehart and Winston.

Berliner, D. C. (2004). Describing the behavior and documenting the accomplishments of expert teachers. *Bulletin of Science, Technology & Society, 24*(3), 200–212.

Bourdieu, P. (1986). The forms of capital. In J. G. Richardson (Ed.), *Handbook of theory and research for the sociology of education* (pp. 241–258). Westport, CT: Greenwood Press.

Bozeman, B., & Feeney, M. K. (2007). Toward a useful theory of mentoring: A conceptual analysis and critique. *Administration & Society, 39*(6), 719–739. doi:10.1177/0095399707304119.

Chase, W. G., & Simon, H. A. (1973). Perception in chess. *Cognitive Psychology, 4*, 55–81.

Chi, M. T. H., Glaser, R., & Farr, M. J. (Eds.). (1988). *The nature of expertise*. Hillsdale, NJ: Lawrence Erlbaum Associates.

Cohen, N. H., & Galbraith, M. W. (1995). Mentoring in the learning society. In M. W. Galbraith & N. H. Cohen (Eds.), *Mentoring: New strategies and challenges* (pp. 5–14). San Francisco, CA: Jossey-Bass.

Coleman, J. S. (1990). *Foundations of social theory*. Cambridge, MA: The Belknap Press of Harvard University Press.

Collins, T., Slough, S., & Waxman, H. (2009). Lessons learned about mentoring junior faculty in higher education. *Academic Leadership, 7*(2), 18–22.

Daloz, L. A. (1999). *Mentor: Guiding the journey of adult learners*. San Francisco, CA: Jossey-Bass.

Dreyfus, H. L., & Dreyfus, S. E. (1986). Five steps from novice to expert. *Mind over machine* (pp. 16–51). New York, NY: Free Press.

Dungy, T. (with Whitaker, N.). (2010). *The mentor leader: Secrets to building people and teams that win consistently*. Carol Stream, IL: Tyndale House Publishers.

Ericsson, K. A., & Hoffman, R. R. (2003). Domain expertise. In J. W. Guthrie (Ed.), *Encyclopedia of education: Vol. 2. common-expertise* (2nd ed., pp. 765–767). New York, NY: Macmillan Reference USA.

Ericsson, K. A., & Smith, J. (Eds.). (1991). *Toward a general theory of expertise*. New York, NY: Cambridge University Press.

Feldman, M. D., Arean, P. A., Marshall, S. J., Lovett, M., & O'Sullivan, P. (2010). Does mentoring matter: Results from a survey of faculty mentees at a large health sciences university. *Medical Education Online, 15*(1), 1–8. doi:10.3402/meo.v15i0.5063

Ghosh, R. (2013). Mentors providing challenge and support: Integrating concepts from teacher mentoring in education and organizational mentoring in business. *Human Resource Development Review, 12*(2), 144–176. doi:10.1177/1534484312465608

Holyoak, K. J. (1991). Symbolic connectionism: Toward third-generation theories of expertise. In K. A. Ericsson & J. Smith (Eds.), *Toward a general theory of expertise* (pp. 301–329). New York, NY: Cambridge University Press.

Jonson, K. F. (2002). *Being an effective mentor: How to help beginning teachers succeed*. Thousand Oaks, CA: Corwin Press.

Johnson, W. B. (2007). *On being a mentor: A guide for higher education faculty*. Mahwah, NJ: Lawrence Erlbaum Associates.

Larkin, J. H. (1979). Processing information for effective problem solving. *Engineering Education, 70*(3), 258–288.

Laverick, D. M. (2005). *A qualitative study of teachers certified by the National Board for Professional Teaching Standards and their expertise in promoting early literacy*. Retrieved from Proquest Information and Learning Company. (UMI Microform 3165958).

Laverick, D. M. (2007). Motivation, metacognition, mentors, and money. Ingredients that support teaching expertise. *Early Childhood Education Journal, 34*(4), 247–249.

Lea, Y. (2011). On mentoring: When the student is ready, the teacher will appear. *International Journal of Learning, 18*(1), 259–268.

Lumpkin, A. (2011). A model for mentoring university faculty. *The Educational Forum, 75*(4), 357–368. doi:10.1080/00131725.2011.602466.

McMahon, S., & Piro, J. (2013). Mentoring in a field experience. *Field Experience Journal, 11*, 18–37.

Nakamura, J., Shernoff, D. J., & Hooker, C. H. (2009). *Good mentoring: Fostering excellent practice in higher education*. San Francisco, CA: Jossey-Bass.

Ortlieb, E. T., Biddix, J. P., & Doepker, G. M. (2010). A collaborative approach to higher education induction. *Active Learning in Higher Education, 11*(2), 109–118. doi:10.1177/1469787410365655

Richter, D., Kunter, M., Lüdtke, O., Klusmann, U., Anders, Y., & Baumert, J. (2013). How different mentoring approaches affect beginning teachers' development in the first year of practice. *Teaching and Teacher Education, 36*, 166–177.

Rodriguez, Y. E. G. (1995). Mentoring to diversity: A multicultural approach. In M. W. Galbraith & N. H. Cohen (Eds.), *Mentoring: New strategies and challenges* (pp. 69–77). San Francisco, CA: Jossey-Bass.

Rowley, J. B. (2006). *Becoming a high performance mentor: A guide to reflection and action*. Thousand Oaks, CA: Corwin Press.

Schrodt, P., Cawyer, C. S., & Sanders, R. (2003). An examination of academic mentoring behaviors and new faculty members' satisfaction with socialization and tenure and promotion processes. *Communication Education, 52*(1), 17–29.

Schulz, S. F. (1995). The benefits of mentoring. In M. W. Galbraith & N. H. Cohen (Eds.), *Mentoring: New strategies and challenges* (pp. 57–67). San Francisco: Jossey-Bass.

Searby, L., & Collins, L. (2010). Mentor and mother hen: Just what I needed as a first year professor. *Advancing Women in Leadership Journal, 30*(20), 1–16.

Starkes, J. L., Deakin, J. M., Allard, F., Hodges, N. J., & Hayes, A. (1996). Deliberate practice in sports: What is it anyway? In K. A. Ericsson (Ed.), *The road to excellence: The acquisition of expert performance in the arts and sciences, sports, and games* (pp. 81–106). Mahwah, NJ: Lawrence Erlbaum.

Sternberg, R. J. (1998). Abilities are forms of developing expertise. *Educational Researcher, 27* (3), 11–20.

Sternberg, R. J. (2001). Giftedness as developing expertise: A theory of the interface between high abilities and achieved excellence. *High Ability Studies, 12*(2), 159–178.

Thurston, L. P., Navarrete, L., & Miller, T. (2009). A ten-year faculty mentoring program: Administrator, mentor, and mentee perspectives. *The International Journal of Learning, 16*(4), 401–415.

Zachary, L. J. (2000). *The mentor's guide: Facilitating effective learning relationships*. San Francisco, CA: Jossey-Bass.

Zeind, C. S., Zdanowicz, M., MacDonald, K., Parkhurst, C., King, C., & Wizwer, P. (2005). Developing a sustainable faculty mentoring program. *American Journal of Pharmaceutical Education, 69*(5), 1–13.

Chapter 2
Mentoring New and Junior Faculty

Abstract This chapter describes the ways in which mentoring supports new faculty in higher education. The chapter discusses the importance of mentors in the transition of new faculty to positions in higher education. An overview of the role of the mentor and protégé is shared, along with research-based tips for building positive mentor-protégé relationships. This chapter covers mentoring programs and provides examples of mentoring new and junior faculty and also shares topics that new and junior faculty members would expect to learn as they seek advice and guidance from their mentors. These topics are ones that mentors can use to provide support and resources for their protégés. The chapter concludes with an overview of mentoring new faculty who are women and those from minoritized racial and ethnic groups.

Keywords Mentoring · Mentoring new faculty · Mentoring junior faculty · Mentoring relationships · Transition to teaching in higher education · Mentoring topics · Mentoring women in higher education · Mentoring faculty from minoritized racial and ethnic groups

2.1 Introduction

The professional literature on mentoring provides a strong rationale for instituting mentoring programs in higher education. For example, a study on the perspectives of administrators, mentors, and protégés on a 10-year mentoring program conducted by Thurston et al. (2009) revealed that "mentoring new faculty into successful and secure colleagues saves money, builds programs, promotes student learning, increases morale, and prevents many types of staffing problems faced in universities" (p. 404). It appears, however, as though formal mentoring programs, although needed, are not typically established at every university. For example, one faculty member explained:

> I have attended three different universities for my undergraduate, masters, and doctoral degrees… None of the universities I attended had formal mentoring programs. The informal mentoring I experienced took many forms, all of which were situational or supervisory in nature, such as: opportunities to write and publish with professors/peers; opportunities to present at conferences with professors/peers; internships. (Heider, personal communication, 2014)

D.M. Laverick, *Mentoring Processes in Higher Education*,
SpringerBriefs in Education, DOI 10.1007/978-3-319-39217-2_2

Heider mentioned that different forms of mentoring took place in various institutions, which suggests that a consistent approach to mentoring is needed. The need for mentoring programs not only benefits the protégés but also institutions of higher education. For example, Thurston et al. (2009) noted that universities that invest in mentoring programs are rewarded with "a stronger presence in research and funding and scholarship, a more dynamic teaching cadre, and an academic team interested in learning, contributing, and growing" (p. 414).

It is important that a formal mentoring program be established and mentors be assigned to new faculty as early in the academic year as possible so that new faculty, including temporary or adjunct faculty, have someone to turn to for assistance and support from the start. While having a mentor assigned upon hiring new faculty may seem optimal, cultivating the naturalness of the mentoring relationship is described by Lea (2011) as a challenge, because "gained respect should be reciprocal, unplanned, beyond a timeline or follow a calendar" (p. 266). Another challenge of mentoring programs relates to pairing new faculty with the right match of a mentor, which is an essential piece of mentoring (Ford, pseudonym, personal communication, 2014). Finding the right match for new faculty is crucial and the assignment of mentors may be made by the department chairperson and/or a mentoring committee. The following recommendation for developing positive mentoring relationships was made by a faculty member who also served as a department chairperson:

> Positive mentoring relationships should be developed by allowing mentors and mentees to choose each other, providing opportunities for collaboration, and creating opportunities for formative evaluations. I believe the Department Chairperson and Assistant Chairperson should mentor everyone, then after a month or so, allow the mentee to choose his or her mentor. The Chairperson can assist by matching mentees with faculty members with similar teaching and research interests. Opportunities for formal activities (like committee work) and informal opportunities (coffee or lunch) should be provided for new and veteran people to meet. (Rieg, personal communication, 2014)

Helterbran shared that she did not have a mentor when she was a temporary faculty member and once she was hired in a tenure-track position, most of the areas in which she would have been mentored were self-discovered as a survival strategy (personal communication, 2014). It is therefore important for temporary faculty, in addition to new tenure-track faculty, to be assigned mentors. For temporary faculty who move among different institutions in search of a tenure-track position, mentoring is critical because "often, new faculty members find it difficult to understand the best approach to take in handling a situation if they do not take into account the culture and unique aspects of the institution" (Zeind et al. 2005, p. 11).

It is with these considerations in mind that the focus of this chapter turns toward the importance of mentors in the transition of new faculty to positions in higher education. The term "new faculty" refers to any faculty member who is hired in a new position in higher education and includes temporary/adjunct faculty.

2.2 The Importance of Mentors in the Transition to Higher Education

New faculty may be faced with challenges that stem from the transition to higher education from their previous work experience. Conrad explained that new faculty "want to fit into the department and need to develop positive relationships with students, colleagues and administrators, along with adjusting to a new community and new role" (pseudonym, personal communication, 2014). Furthermore,

> Higher education is unique, so there are certain aspects that could not have been experienced in another venue. Mentoring is important because people are going through things for the first time at many stages of their lives. All people need support in all aspects of their journeys. (Sibert, personal communication, 2014)

In these situations, the role of the mentor is crucial. Furthermore, a mentor "lowers the rate of turnover, increases the quality of success, provides a neutral person to seek answers to questions, and helps to eliminate the amount of error with new hires" (Marcoline, personal communication, 2014).

A faculty member who was previously a school teacher and administrator believed that because she had not worked full-time in a university setting, she therefore had a large amount of information to learn in a short period of time in order to function effectively (Sibert, personal communication, 2014). This sentiment was echoed by Conrad who shared:

> I accepted the fact that higher education was new territory for me and that my limited knowledge of the culture and expectations of my new role would require professional and personal support. Specifically, I needed to ask many questions and not feel like I was a burden to those that were very familiar, but had many responsibilities of their own. (pseudonym, personal communication, 2014)

Similarly, the immersion of a former principal and superintendent into higher education was facilitated through mentoring. He stated,

> The culture and routine responsibilities are vastly different from public education. Although I was a school principal and superintendent for many years, the teaching responsibilities in higher education require a full immersion into the university setting. My contact with higher education had been limited in my previous positions, mostly to that of a student. Now, trying to get a full understanding of how higher education functions, the advisory role of professors, and the minutia of that of a classroom teacher can be daunting. Fortunately, a department colleague stepped forward in spite of no formal mentoring program. Needless to say, having a go-to person was a big help! (Marcoline, personal communication, 2014)

Another faculty member, with a similar background, explained the importance of mentoring:

> Without successful mentoring, the first year experience for an incoming faculty member may be more difficult than necessary. A positive first year should become the foundation for a positive career at the university. It should not be a negative experience that has to be overcome in subsequent years in order for a faculty member to have a sound understanding of the requirements of his or her position. (Frantz, personal communication, 2014)

Wen explained that mentoring makes new instructors feel more secure and less likely to feel at loss with the proper approaches to teaching new courses. Further, he shared that mentoring saves the time for new instructors to map out the outline of the pedagogy for certain courses, which helps to avoid a trial and error approach by new instructors that may negatively impact the students (personal communication, 2014). A faculty member offered this perspective:

> Mentoring in higher education is important because higher education is unlike any other profession of which I am aware. Where else do you have a full-time job where you are only *required* to be at your workplace 17 hours per week? New faculty members must learn the trilogy of teaching, scholarship, and service, and how to manage/balance time to be successful and earn tenure and promotions. Without effective mentors, novice faculty members are doomed to fail. The 17 hours someone is required to be at the workplace may be in the evenings when no one else is "on the floor" or on weekends at an off-campus location. It is difficult to develop relationships if your schedule is one where you are not working when your colleagues are on campus. A good mentor can help with retention of new faculty members and assist them as they teach, publish, and serve. (Rieg, personal communication, 2014)

The notion of balancing the expectations associated with teaching, scholarship, and service, is an important one for mentors to address with protégés. For example, junior faculty may be overburdened with preparing new courses and advising students that they do not find time to engage in scholarship (Collins et al. 2009). Collins and colleagues advised that junior faculty limit their class preparation to a fixed amount of time to assist with this concern. Additionally, a formalized plan for mentoring new faculty in their development as researchers and academicians is needed (Zeind et al. 2005). Finding opportunities for service at all levels (e.g., university, college, department, and community) is a role that Infinity played as a mentor for newer faculty members (pseudonym, personal communication, 2014). Mentors need to help their protégés "discriminate between valuable, rewarding service, and less productive and time-consuming opportunities" (Ulery, Sammis, and Mexal, 2004 p. 48).

2.3 Mentoring Programs and Examples of Mentoring New and Junior Faculty

A successful mentoring program needs to be in place in order to facilitate the success of new and junior faculty. According to Paquette, while most mentoring is done informally, a positive step would be to implement a formalized mentoring program so that all new faculty can have similar experiences (personal communication, 2014). Zeind et al. (2005) described the following as keys of a successful mentoring program:

> The formation of a group committed to faculty mentoring (mentorship subcommittee), the support and commitment of administration, the buy-in of senior faculty members and protégés, and the design of the program to support the mission of the academic units and institution. (p. 13)

Successful mentoring programs should show evidence of the following: "(1) positive thinking among all participants; (2) a strong cohort of mentees and mentors; (3) tracking and data collection to document success and failures; (4) objectives documenting clinical or internship experiences; and (5) long-term analysis on the careers of mentees" (Vega et al., 2010, p. 54).

The absence of structured mentoring programs is a disservice to new university faculty. A new faculty member recalled that some colleagues would help her out when she asked for assistance, particularly when teaching a new course or when she had questions about advising students. She recalled learning things mostly through self-discovery and then following up by asking questions, which occurred mostly with university policies and procedures. One way that she was mentored was though her colleagues sharing materials for new courses and assisting with advisement. As a tenured faculty member, she now mentors new faculty in her department in these ways (Ford, personal communication, 2014).

To avoid a haphazard approach to mentoring, it is important to look to the professional literature on successful mentoring programs and strategies that may be used to support new and junior faculty through mentoring. In 2011, Lumpkin reviewed the literature on successful mentoring programs in order to propose a model that includes the following four stages: conceptualization, design and development, implementation, and evaluation. She noted that potential benefits of this model include socialization into the culture, emotional support, networking, and increased job performance.

The key characteristics of mentoring programs identified in Lumpkin's (2011) review include: "defining a clear purpose, goals, and strategies; selecting, matching, and preparing protégés and mentors for their new roles; holding regular meetings to nurture interactions among protégés and mentors; and evaluating program effectiveness" (p. 358). Some highlights of the key characteristics that Lumpkin described for each of these components are as follows:

- Defining a clear purpose, goals, and strategies: A campus-wide group that is representative should develop a succinct purpose statement. Additionally, administrators need to demonstrate commitment in this initial phase.
- Selecting, matching, and preparing protégés and mentors: The advisory committee develops a program handbook, advertises the program, gives mentors and protégés opportunities to request professional development programs, and allows them to be actively involved in the matching process.
- Holding regular meetings and interactions: Time is needed in order to capitalize on the benefits of mentoring.
- Evaluating the effectiveness of mentoring programs: Formative and summative evaluations that include quantitative and qualitative measures were recommended.

The discussion will now turn toward important considerations for mentoring, some of which echo Lumpkin's research findings. These ideas include: assigning mentors and timing, professional development and evaluation of mentoring programs, and promoting ongoing communication and positive interactions.

2.3.1 Assignment of Mentors and Timing

Once new faculty are hired, the assignment of mentors is the initial step in helping them become acclimated into their new position and promoting a successful transition. The formal mentoring program should assign veteran faculty mentors to temporary/adjunct faculty as well as tenure-track faculty and consider the mentoring needs of each protégé with mentors assigned who will engage with protégés to collaborate on projects.

A study conducted by Thurston et al. (2009) found that the ways in which mentors meet the needs of their protégés differ from year to year with each protégé. Therefore, mentoring should to be individualized to meet each protégé's needs and the matching process should address these needs. A formal mentoring program could be set up to match mentors with protégés through an online database that would share mentoring needs, mentor characteristics, etc. (Ford, pseudonym, personal communication, 2014). Another approach is to have the mentors and protégés involved in coordinating the mentoring assignments in order to promote greater ownership of the relationship; however, research has shown that some faculty needed assistance in finding mentors (Feldman et al. 2010).

It is important to have mentors act as designated contact persons for protégés to consult and ask questions. Mentors may then direct protégés to other persons or resources as needed. Having more than one mentor has been recommended (Diggs et al. 2009; Feldman et al. 2010) and depending on the needs of the protégé, mentors help support them according to those needs. The University of California, San Francisco's mentoring program in health sciences encourages junior faculty to "assemble a mentoring team consisting of a career mentor, scholarly mentor, and co-mentor with clear roles and responsibilities" (Feldman et al. 2010, p. 6). According to these researchers the career mentor is a "senior faculty member primarily responsible for providing career guidance and support" (p. 6); the scholarly mentor "must be an expert in the scientific or scholarly area of the mentee" (p. 6); and the co-mentor is "responsible for working with the lead mentor on overall mentoring responsibilities… for the mentee and for providing particular guidance in their area of expertise" (p. 6). Kawalilak and Groen (2010) described co-mentoring as a way for new faculty to support one another. They advised that new faculty should "tend to one's pre-tenure journey by creating a safe reflective space to step back from challenges of being a new academic" (p. 143). It is from this space, they explain, that co-mentoring may evolve. With regard to having a safe environment, it was recommended that the mentor should create an environment in which perfection is not expected from new and junior faculty but rather personal and professional growth (Johnson, personal communication, 2014). This perspective is important given that the transition to higher education from another position can present a new, and challenging, learning experience.

Once mentor-protégé matches have been made, the mentoring relationships should "last longer than one year, be formal in nature, be based upon an assignment with a competent tenured employee, and exist for the needs of both the institution and new employee. The mentor should also receive some type of recognition or compensation" (Marcoline, personal communication, 2014).

Concerns about the ways in which institutions organize mentoring programs were shared by Lea (2011):

> The institutional will's dominance over the mentor/apprenticeships truncates the natural grown affinity… as a result, most mentoring programs are created for a skill-based transient existence via workshops, speaking events, discussion circles, etc. Institutional formality and programming can merely be a bad imitation of nature. Its attempt to replicate is obtrusive against the naturalness in building trust and independent decision making to mentor and to be a mentee. Mentoring empowers and affirms the seeker for self-actualization. The need to claiming the authority of ones' own mind stipulates taking ownership of the means and control for knowledge production. Mentoring is essentially teaching to live with freedom. (p. 264)

2.3.2 Professional Development and Evaluation of Mentoring Programs

Participation in professional development workshops was a recommendation made by Collins et al. (2009) for mentors to renew best practices for their role. The professional development activities should focus on growth, not remediation, according to Collins et al. While professional development experiences help faculty improve their practice, it is also important to evaluate the successfulness of mentoring programs and make continual improvements based on ongoing evaluation.

The following quote illustrates the importance of using a cyclical approach to mentoring new faculty, which serves as a method to continually evaluating and improving the mentoring process:

> I believe after the initial year in the position, each new faculty member should meet to discuss his/her first year with the department chairperson. At that meeting, it could be valuable to the chairperson to hear both the positives and negatives of that new employee's experiences in order to share good ideas and positive experiences as well as suggestions for improvement on the mentoring process for future new faculty and mentors. It stands to reason; if one new employee had concerns or questions on a procedure, process, or teaching requirement, then another will most likely have similar questions. By debriefing after one year in the position, I feel some of those concerns and issues may be addressed for incoming faculty. That information could be shared in a type of FAQ sheet that could be given to all mentors and new faculty members. That document could serve as a starting point for the initial mentoring meeting and also serve as a place for the new faculty member to reference when looking for departmental or university information. (Frantz, personal communication, 2014)

Cohen (1995) proposed the need for mentor self-assessment. He cautioned against "placing too much focus on analyzing the performance of the person in the student role (mentee) and too little focus understanding the importance of the individual in the teacher role (mentor)" (p. 16). Furthermore, Cohen stated,

> If the mentoring experience is to truly benefit the mentee, training programs must avoid an imbalance of emphasis on the significant contribution of the mentor, an imbalance that could seriously limit the enriched learning opportunities that derive as much from mentor initiatives as from mentee responses and actions. (p. 16)

Blood and colleagues (2012) recommended that mentoring programs need to take into account the developmental and situational stages in careers and that mentors should be trained to ask protégés specifically about these areas because the mentoring needs of faculty vary according to academic rank, duration at rank, research focus, and parenting status. Once mentors identify specific areas in which their protégés need support, the mentors can work with department chairs to provide assistance as needed. For example, in terms of parenting status, Paquette elaborated that newly hired faculty should have attention given to their schedules, including consideration of travel requirements and the assignment of teaching evenings and weekend classes (personal communication, 2014).

2.3.3 *Promoting Ongoing Communication and Positive Interactions*

The importance of the mentor taking an interest in the protégé's personal life, as well as professional life was shared by Paquette (personal communication, 2014). This type of relationship developed into a friendship, which will always be important to her. Lasting friendships is a benefit of mentoring as described by Infinity (pseudonym, personal communication, 2014). These examples highlight the importance of promoting ongoing communication and positive interactions. This section will describe ways in which mentors may promote these types of interactions.

A strategy that was deemed successful by a new faculty member involved meeting with her mentor for lunch on a monthly basis (Infiniti, pseudonym, personal communication, 2014). To prepare for these meetings, Infiniti would write her questions in a notebook to be answered when she met with her mentor. It appears as though this strategy of writing down questions prior to mentoring meetings could help with addressing an apparent gap between what mentors and protégés believe to be important topics of discussion. For example, Feldman et al. (2010) found:

> While only 28% of mentees reported reviewing their promotion/merit packet with their mentor, it was the top-rated topic that mentees said they wanted assistance with. Likewise, only 31% reported discussing issues of personal-professional balance with their mentor but it was in the top five topics for which mentees reporting wanting assistance. (p. 6)

Furthermore, Feldman et al. speculated that mentors might define their mentoring role more narrowly than protégés do.

Collins et al. (2009) offered the following suggestions for mentoring activities that would support junior faculty: (1) informal dinner circles with colleagues that promote conversations about similar interests and their work; (2) mentoring lunches in which mentor/protégé pairs meet; and (3) forums in which junior faculty get to see and hear about their colleagues' work. Furthermore, as shared by Murray, an informal relationship that is non-evaluative should be encouraged (personal communication, 2014).

The amount of time that it takes to nurture mentoring relationships cannot be underestimated; therefore, the concept of having multiple mentors can assist with this challenge. Collins and colleagues (2009) noted that "having more mentors with more specialized roles allows the new faculty member to seek out help without overburdening a single individual and increase the likelihood of success for individual tasks and career goals" (para 18). Having more than one mentor would help address the challenge of finding enough time for effective mentorship by one individual. Furthermore, having multiple mentors would address some of the challenges that might be encountered when only one mentor is assigned. Rieg shared these ideas and challenges:

> The biggest challenge I faced as a mentee and mentor was TIME. Because of conflicting schedules it is often difficult to find the time to meet as a mentor and mentee. It is important to MAKE face-to-face time for mentoring, put it on my calendar, and do not let other meetings or people interfere with that commitment. Another challenge is when formal mentors and mentees do not 'click'... Another challenge in my department is the lack of diversity – new candidates from minority groups often seek mentors from outside our department (which isn't necessarily a bad thing but it sometimes isolates people). It is difficult to recruit and retain diverse faculty members. The benefits of mentoring far outweigh the challenges! (personal communication, 2014)

Because effective mentoring requires commitment and time, those who organize mentoring programs need to consider the workload in order to have an adequate number of mentors (Zeind et al. 2005). A participant in the study conducted by Ortlieb et al. (2010) explained that a challenge he faced as a new faculty member related to "developing close relationships with faculty who were already overburdened with duties and responsibilities" (p. 115). It has been recommended that in order "to make mentoring a more sustainable and profitable practice, mentors should receive appropriate training, resources and rewards from the administration to demonstrate support for the program" (Ulery et al. 2004, p. 48).

2.4 Topics of Importance for New and Junior Faculty

The specific needs of each new faculty member must be taken into account in order for the mentor to tailor the mentoring process to meet the protégé's individual needs. Determining a plan of action may be the result of discussing the particular challenges that each new faculty member faces. For example, a new faculty member shared his experience:

> After working in public education for 36 years, I found I had to learn an entire new set of rules and procedures. This was necessary in addition to the time consuming preparation required to begin teaching new classes. At times, even with my experience and maturity, it

> was overwhelming. To overcome this, I worked with my mentor through emails, in person, and during an occasional lunch to address all my questions and concerns. In addition, I talked with the department chairperson and several faculty members who had either taught my courses prior to me or had experience from longevity in their positions. I aligned myself to "positive individuals" who had the information I needed to succeed and the time and willingness to share that information. (Frantz, personal communication, 2014)

Rather than assuming what protégés need, mentors should be certain to ask their protégés what their mentoring needs are in order to help them be successful. A more formal approach would be to give a needs assessment in order to help identify specific challenges and then tailor mentoring experiences to the unique needs of new and junior faculty. For example, one new faculty member felt comfortable with teaching yet fearful about conducting research and publishing (Searby and Collins 2010). Additionally, mentors should support their protégés through the tenure and promotion processes (Murray, personal communication, 2014). Zeind et al. (2005) advised that "colleges and universities should tailor faculty development and mentoring to the collective and individual needs of the institution and the academic units" (p. 13). Generally, mentoring should be provided to help new faculty "understand the requirements and expectations of teaching, scholarship, service, and fulfilment of professional responsibilities" (Paquette, personal communication, 2014). It is important that mentors understand the particular needs of junior faculty in order to provide the appropriate level of support. Collins et al. (2009) explained,

> Today's junior faculty in many colleges are often older and more likely to be female, ethnic minorities, or foreign born. These facts alone make the lived experienced [*sic*] of junior faculty very different than the experiences that the tenured, white-male faculty member or administrator had perhaps decades ago. (para 2)

The mentor of one faculty member who experienced early success in higher education provided "the framework for open sharing of information about tenure and promotion expectations, the inside politics of the department and school, and research protocols at the university" (Searby and Collins 2010, p. 2). Participants in a study conducted by Schrodt et al. (2003) found that participants expressed a need for additional support with research and university politics. They also commented that their findings emphasized the importance of new faculty receiving information from those inside the organization. A common topic for mentors and protégés was also found to be securing funding (Feldman et al. 2010).

Another common topic that should be addressed is the need for support with writing for publication. According to a former public school teacher and administrator, having an accomplished writer support her in co-authoring publications addressed this need (Helterbran, personal communication, 2014). Paquette elaborated on how her mentor assisted her with scholarship by sharing some of her publications and talking with her about the publication process (personal communication, 2014). Furthermore, Paquette's scholarship was supported by co-writing with another faculty member who was hired at the same time. The need for mentorship in writing for publication was echoed by Infinity (pseudonym, personal communication, 2014) who noted that this requirement was not an expectation in her previous role. A faculty member who was a prolific writer invited her to co-author a book and then mentored her through the writing process. This mentorship led to improved confidence in writing and improved writing skills.

In addition to learning about writing for publication, learning the procedures within the department and university are needs expressed by new faculty. One new faculty member reported that she learned these procedures by talking to colleagues and asking questions; she felt that colleagues mentored her by allowing her to attend meetings and do a lot of listening. She also felt that sometimes she just needed a kind face and a friendly word, which mentoring provided her with at many times during many days. She further mentioned that while having a designated mentor was important, she additionally sought the assistance of others (Sibert, personal communication, 2014).

To summarize some of the procedural aspects of mentoring new faculty, Frantz (personal communication, 2014) shared the following examples of topics that mentors could address with their protégés:

- Writing a course syllabus (share samples)
- Selecting and ordering textbooks
- Determining a grading scale
- Accessing campus resources for faculty and students, such as the services that a Writing Center, research facility, and library provide
- Conducting student evaluations (e.g., share a sample of the evaluation prior to the start of the new faculty member's first semester of teaching)
- Securing instructional supplies
- Scheduling office hours
- Entering course data for accreditation purposes
- Advising students and assisting them with scheduling and completing (and evaluation of) electronic portfolios
- Observing and evaluating student teachers (i.e., share examples of completed observations and evaluation forms; explain requirements for Teacher Work Samples; and certification procedures)
- Grading policies and procedures for entering mid-term and final grades
- Preparing for evaluation (i.e., teaching, scholarship, and service expectations; preparation of portfolio or binder of supporting documentation and evaluation forms)
- Scheduling and conducting peer observations
- Earning tenure (i.e., process and requirements)
- Requesting vehicles for official travel
- Requesting the use of personal and sick days
- Securing a parking permit

Mentors need to carefully consider what information is given and when because, according to Collins et al. (2009), giving too much information to junior faculty before they actually need to use and implement procedures might be detrimental because without implementation the procedures may not make sense. If the mentor has experienced similar situations as a new faculty member, they may draw on their experiences to determine what information is needed when. Frantz elaborated by sharing:

> A mentor should be an individual who has either taught one of the courses the new faculty member is teaching or has a working understanding of the course or program. Although the sharing of basic departmental information and procedures is important, the new faculty member was hired to teach. Therefore, information related to teaching specific courses in a higher education setting should be the highest priority in the mentoring process.

New faculty may feel pressure in trying to balance teaching with other responsibilities such as advisement, scholarship, and service. A participant in a study conducted by Ortlieb et al. (2010) explained that his greatest challenge as a new faculty member was advising students, in addition to the pressure of needing publish. In the same study, another participant shared that his challenges related to determining which meetings were considered mandatory and which were suggested and how this determination related to the organizational culture. He also felt challenged in establishing a research agenda.

Given the previous information, the discussion will now turn toward some specific topics that are common areas of concern for new faculty. These topics include observations, writing syllabi, student evaluations, scholarship, and tenure and promotion.

2.4.1 *Observations*

As a requirement for tenure and evaluation purposes, new faculty are required to be observed. The feedback provided as a result of these observations may be very useful and help focus the protégé's efforts to grow as an instructor in higher education. An observation-and-conference cycle for mentoring new teachers, proposed by Jonson (2008), can be a useful tool in higher education. Jonson described this cycle as: (1) preobservation conference, in which the mentor and protégé determine the observation's focus; (2) observation, which involves the mentor "intentionally and methodically observing interaction" (p. 121) and recording data; and (3) postobservation conference, in which the focus of the observation is shared with the protégé and feedback is provided.

From a mentoring perspective, observations should be conducted on a mutual basis. Specifically, protégés would benefit from the opportunity to observe their mentors and other faculty teach, according to Conrad (pseudonym, personal communication, 2014). She explained,

> I was looking for specific feedback to improve my teaching. I asked for resources and suggestions, and was provided with resources and ideas that were shared with me to support me. I wanted to ask for more opportunities to observe my peers to get ideas.

Zachary (2000) stated,

> There is no greater contribution to mentee learning than the gift a mentor provides by giving and receiving ongoing, honest, constructive feedback. Expanding the capacity of a mentee to do the same promotes competence, inspires confidence, and enriches the learning experience. (p. 136)

This quote supports the idea put forth by Conrad that in addition to being observed by a mentor, the protégé should also have the opportunity to observe the mentor and use this opportunity as a learning experience. Murray believes the mentor-protégé relationship to be non-evaluative and explained that the mentor can be a champion for the protégé (personal communication, 2015). Furthermore, Thurston and colleagues (2009) explained,

> Openness and honesty are needed to build trust, so that the mentee can feel free to share questions, concerns, and overall fears. Both the mentor and the mentee need to be able to express divergent opinions as they work together. (p. 405)

2.4.2 Syllabi

When mentors share examples of syllabi with their protégés, they are providing another level of support. By sharing high quality syllabi, mentors may explain terminology and the thinking that went into their creation (Conrad, pseudonym, personal communication, 2014).

2.4.3 Student Evaluations

For new faculty, the need to gain positive student evaluations is a reality that they must confront. New faculty may be challenged by teaching new courses and therefore become concerned about the effect of lack of experience on student evaluations. Therefore, mentors should spend time reviewing the student evaluation instrument at the onset of the semester and help the protégé focus on strategies that may be implemented to meet the intended goals of the evaluation process.

2.4.4 Scholarship

Ford shared that she mentors new faculty by offering to collaborate with them on projects, publishing, and research (pseudonym, personal communication, 2014). Collaboration with new faculty can be a double-edged sword, however, as shared by one faculty member:

> I do believe that my strong collaborative nature and mentoring nature has often been to my own professional detriment. When I look at what I have done, I realize that by inviting

> others along I often have to share the credit which is not so good for promotion. (Ford, pseudonym, personal communication, 2014)

This idea relates to the previous discussion on having enough time for effective mentoring and recognition of the time that mentors spend to support their protégés. It appears that if the level of scholarship in which mentors engage decreases as a result of mentoring, the higher education institution should hold mentorship of new faculty in higher esteem. In other words, co-publishing between a mentor and a protégé should hold the same level of significance as manuscripts that are solely published.

2.4.5 Tenure and Promotion

Taken collectively, peer observations, creating syllabi, student evaluations, and scholarship lead to one of the most important topics of concern for new faculty members: tenure and promotion. The role of the mentor is critical for helping new faculty become tenured and promoted. Ford (pseudonym) confided:

> I think egos and the pressure for tenure and promotion are difficult and a good mentor *that you can trust* can help keep you grounded, focused and help manage stress and anxiety. The *"oh this will be good for tenure"* can really overwhelm you. A good mentor will help you wade through what really is and is not 'good for tenure' so you are not so overcommitted. (personal communication, 2014)

Since she has earned tenure and has been promoted, Ford helps new faculty by sharing how evaluation materials were organized. By doing so, she provides a model that shows new faculty the expectation of what applying for promotion entails.

Ford elaborated by explaining her work with securing grants and how this type of scholarship, while personally gratifying, is not as valued when being considered for promotion. She is constantly encouraged by her department to do grant work with no release, which consumes much of her time. She shared, "I wish I had a mentor who has followed a similar path to help me navigate this avenue of scholarship because it is rewarding and reaches far more people than some obscure publication or book but is not as valued" (pseudonym, personal communication, 2014). Ford's experience aligns with the work of Kawalilak and Groen (2010) who advised that new faculty should "tend to one's pre-tenure journey by creating a safe reflective space to step back from challenges of being a new academic" (p. 143). Mentors who have experienced the pressures that new faculty face are best positioned to help their protégés in this regard.

Collins et al. (2009) suggested that evaluation procedures for junior faculty need not be identical to tenured faculty and advised that undifferentiated procedures do not support junior faculty's professional development.

2.5 Mentoring New and Junior Faculty that Include Women and Minoritized Racial and Ethnic Groups

New and junior faculty who are women or those who are from minoritized racial and ethnic groups have unique needs that may be met through mentoring. This section will discuss first the mentoring needs of female new and junior and faculty before turning toward the needs of those from minoritized racial and ethnic groups.

2.5.1 *New and Junior Faculty Who Are Women*

While new faculty members need support in order to be successful in higher education, women often fend for themselves as they enter the academy (Searby and Collins 2010). Women have unique mentoring needs that make it good to talk with other women who face similar responsibilities (Layton, pseudonym, personal communication, 2015). A study of women medical school faculty found that 54 % of the participants reported having a mentor but that a significant number had unmet mentoring needs (Blood et al. 2012). A unique need that Infinity expressed relates to her belief that new faculty need to learn how to succeed in an atmosphere that could be deemed an "all boys' club" at times and in some situations (pseudonym, personal communication, 2014). This idea aligns with the work of Searby and Collins (2010) who explained that new faculty who are women are often left to fend for themselves. To address this concern, putting more females in leadership roles may be helpful. In terms of mentoring, matching female mentors and protégés with similar interests and backgrounds may be effective. The needs expressed by women faculty at the assistant professor rank with regard to mentoring include writing and publishing articles (Blood et al. 2012). Infinity has had experience mentoring male and female colleagues and believes that men have unique mentoring needs as well, likely due to their previous professional experiences prior to entering the university setting as faculty.

2.5.2 *New and Junior Faculty from Minoritized Racial and Ethnic Groups*

The term "minoritized" racial and ethnic groups is used in this publication in keeping with the terminology shared in *Is Everyone Really Equal?* (Sensoy and DiAngelo 2011). Sensoy and DiAngelo defined a minoritized group as:

> A social group that is devalued in society. This devaluing encompasses how the group is represented, what degree of access to resources it is granted, and how the unequal access is rationalized. Traditionally, a group in this position has been referred to as the *minority group*. However, this language has been replaced with the term *minoritized* in order to

> capture the active dynamics that create the lower status in society and also to signal that the group's status is not necessarily related to how many or few of them there are in the population at large. (p. 186)

In terms of mentoring in higher education, the definition offered by Sensoy and DiAngelo points to the importance of insuring access to mentoring as a resource to support minoritized groups in the higher education community. Rodriguez (1995) cautioned, "Many values held and assumptions made within a Western, male, upper-middle-class construct may not be applicable, and instead of promoting multiple perspectives, may lead to mentoring that aims for homogenization or conformity to one viewpoint" (p. 76). Furthermore, according to Diggs et al. (2009), "Predominately White institutions have not yet realized their goals of recruiting and retaining faculty of color in meaningful numbers" (p. 330). These authors explained that this issue could be addressed through the mentoring process for minority faculty.

Rodriguez (1995) described multicultural mentoring as "an active process that is deeply contextualized" and developmental (p. 75). She cautioned that since many mentors were educated in monocultural environments, they need to "become multicultural people before they can address mentoring to diversity" (p. 75). Citing Nieto's (1992) three-step process (1992), Rodriguez offered these steps: (1) learn more; (2) confront your own racism and bias; and (3) learn to see reality from a variety of perspectives.

At the community college level, Vega et al. (2010) noted that "a formal mentoring project for minority faculty must be accountable and backed up with reliable data to have a systemic and sustainable effect over time" (pp. 53–54). Additionally, Vega et al. recommended that a mentoring program for minority faculty at a community college includes: "mentoring by a well-respected practitioner; job shadowing; clinical or internship experiences; and time spent in the daily life and activities of the culture of the community college" (p. 54). These authors wrote about the need for community colleges to recruit and retain a diverse faculty. Implementing best practices in mentoring is a step in meeting this need.

Frazier (2011) advised universities to create mentoring programs in which African American scholars serve as mentors at the institution or through other organizations that can provide a network for mentoring African American faculty who are untenured. Specifically, she recommended that mentoring programs at universities must be created in which African American scholars serve as mentors through a network of mentoring African American faculty who are untenured. According to Vega et al. (2010), "Successful mentoring for minority faculty and administrators must be: credible, reliable, systemic and structured, highly regarded, focused on outcomes, and associated with a credible organization or institution" (p. 54).

The participants in a study conducted by Diggs et al. (2009) shared that that faculty of color do not necessarily need to have a mentor who is a cultural match. Tillman's (2001) study examined the mentoring relationships between African American faculty who were nontenured, with the exception of one, and their senior faculty mentors who, for the most part, were White. Tillman stated,

> Same-race match is likely to be the strongest predictor of success in a mentor-protégé relationship, and most mentor-protégé relationships tend to be same-race rather than cross-race relationships; however, all of the protégés in this study, except one, had White primary mentors. The majority of these protégés, as well as the mentors, emphasized that the essence of their relationship was mentoring for professional growth and development and that the most important factor was whether the mentors could provide the protégés with the kind of career support necessary to achieve promotion and tenure. All of the protégés agreed that race could, at times, be a factor that affected the relationship on a personal/cultural level, but they expressed few concerns about race as a factor in their professional relationship. (p. 313)

A different perspective was offered by Evans and Packer-Williams (2011) who advised that "mentees may feel suspicious of and behave more awkwardly around mentors who are different from them" (p. 9). Evans and Packer-Williams reported the results of their study of a group of African American junior faculty at a traditionally White institution who formed a peer mentoring group in which they assisted each other in growing as new professors. This group, according to the authors, believed that their peer mentoring program was effective for mentoring African American women faculty and advised that administrators in higher education should consider creating such mentoring programs. Evans and Packer-Williams found that peer mentoring in this program acted as a vehicle for the participants to process and cope effectively with microaggressions; helped the participants increase positive self-identity and self-efficacy as a scholar; and recognized and helped participants recognize and combat internalized oppression and stereotypes.

The participants in the study conducted by Diggs et al. (2009) suggested that having more than one mentor is beneficial due to the various experiences, resources, and support that they may offer. This approach worked for Infinity because her "assigned mentor" moved away after her first year in higher education and from that point on, she was mentored by a variety of faculty in leadership roles in her department (e.g., department chairperson, student teaching coordinator, program coordinator, etc.) (pseudonym, personal communication, 2014). Whereas Infinity met formally in monthly meetings with her assigned mentor, after her first year the various mentors didn't meet formally with her but rather answered questions as they arose. Sibert advised that the best way to support one another involves time and talking, whether the situation is related to race, gender, or ethnicity (personal communication, 2014). Rodriguez (1995) advised,

> For mentoring to be a change agent for the institution as well as the person being mentored, the assumptions underlying traditional models of hierarchical mentoring must be challenged to allow for democratic participation in the institution as well as in the society at large. A vision of mentoring that emphasizes the acceptance of differences as enriching the worldview and contributions of an institution could transform mentoring practices, making them congruent with our diverse society. (p. 76)

Diggs et al. (2009) found that faculty of color desired the "establishment of a community of scholars of color as an important support for their work" in which participants collaborate on research and exchange ideas (p. 324). The researchers explained,

> Mentoring activities helped to establish a safe place where faculty of color could meet" and that safe place was a "*colored space*; a space where minority faculty could relate to one another beyond the scrutiny of the dominant culture or the shackles of mainstream expectations. (p. 328)

Furthermore, "These kinds of spaces may be of particular importance for faculty who feel that they have to present the smiling face in the public academy while pursuing tenure" (p. 330). While the participants in Tillman's (2001) study

> were successful because of their ability to adapt to and negotiate the mainstream academic culture… it seems clear that despite their ability to adapt, some of the protégés felt they were outsiders in their institutions and that success, in and of itself, did not necessarily translate into a feeling of belonging. Thus, the culture of the academy, to some extent, may influence the African American faculty member's perception of their acceptance in this institution. (p. 317)

Identifying the mentoring needs of any given university is essential in making mentoring successful. For example, Infinity stated that for a university that is in a predominantly White, middle class town, minority groups face challenges (pseudonym, personal communication, 2014). She elaborated that one reason is that there are not a lot of opportunities for them to socialize with members of their ethnic or racial groups and also that if English is not their native language, students claim that they can't understand them and therefore can't relate to them. In order to address these needs, more social and culturally responsive activities should be provided; background in multicultural education and culturally responsive teaching is needed; and there is a need to learn to appreciate and support ALL people.

Tillman (2001) maintained that institutions must go beyond recruiting African American faculty and take the steps needed to be responsible for their success. Tillman's recommendations for practice include: (1) give consideration as to how mentors will be assigned to new African American faculty, especially with regard to research interests; (2) monitor and evaluate the mentoring relationships; (3) devise a list of the career and psychosocial functions that new faculty need; and (4) seek African American mentors from inside and outside the institution.

References

Blood, E. A., Ullrich, N. J., Hirshfeld-Becker, D. R., Seely, E. W., Connelly, M. T., Warfield, C. A. & Emans, S. J. (2012). Academic women faculty: Are they finding the mentoring they need? *Journal of Women's Health, 21*(11), 1201–1208. doi:10.1089/jwh.2012.3529

Cohen, N. H. (1995). The principles of adult mentoring scale. In M. W. Galbraith & N. H. Cohen (Eds.), *Mentoring: New strategies and challenges* (pp. 15–32). San Francisco, CA: Jossey-Bass.

Collins, T., Slough, S., & Waxman, H. (2009). Lessons learned about mentoring junior faculty in higher education. *Academic Leadership, 7*(2), 18–22.

Diggs, G. A., Garrison-Wade, D. F., Estrada, D., & Galindo, R. (2009). Smiling faces and colored spaces: The experiences of faculty of color pursuing tenure in the academy. *Urban Review, 41*, 312–333. doi:10.1007/s11256-008-0113-y

Evans, K. M., & Packer-Williams, C. L. (2011). Retaining and reclaiming ourselves: Reflections on a peer mentoring group experience or new African American women professors. *Perspectives in Peer Programs, 23*(1), 9–23.

Feldman, M. D., Arean, P. A., Marshall, S. J., Lovett, M., & O'Sullivan, P. (2010). Does mentoring matter: Results from a survey of faculty mentees at a large health sciences university. *Medical Education Online, 15*(1), 1–8. doi:10.3402/meo.v15i0.5063

Frazier, K. N. (2011). Academic bullying: A barrier to tenure and promotion for African-American faculty. *Florida Journal of Educational Administration and Policy, 5*(1), 1–13.

Jonson, K. F. (2008). Practical strategies for assisting new teachers. In C. Press (Ed.), *Mentoring, coaching, and collaboration* (pp. 107–136). Thousand Oaks, CA: Sage.

Kawalilak, C., & Groen, J. (2010). Illuminating the tenure-track pathway: A "new" faculty perspective. *Journal of Educational Thought, 44*(1), 131–146.

Lea, Y. (2011). On mentoring: When the student is ready, the teacher will appear. *International Journal of Learning, 18*(1), 259–268.

Lumpkin, A. (2011). A model for mentoring university faculty. *The Educational Forum, 75*(4), 357–368. doi:10.1080/00131725.2011.602466

Nieto, S. (1992). *Affirming diversity: The socio-political context of multicultural education.* White Plains, NY: Longman.

Ortlieb, E. T., Biddix, J. P., & Doepker, G. M. (2010). A collaborative approach to higher education induction. *Active Learning in Higher Education, 11*(2), 109–118. doi:10.1177/1469787410365655

Rodriguez, Y. E. G. (1995). Mentoring to diversity: A multicultural approach. In M. W. Galbraith & N. H. Cohen (Eds.), *Mentoring: New strategies and challenges* (pp. 69–77). San Francisco, CA: Jossey-Bass.

Schrodt, P., Cawyer, C. S., & Sanders, R. (2003). An examination of academic mentoring behaviors and new faculty members' satisfaction with socialization and tenure and promotion processes. *Communication Education, 52*(1), 17–29.

Searby, L., & Collins, L. (2010). Mentor and mother hen: Just what I needed as a first year professor. *Advancing Women in Leadership Journal, 30*(20), 1–16.

Sensoy, Ö, & DiAngelo, R. (2011). *Is everyone really equal*? New York, NY: Teachers College Press.

Thurston, L. P., Navarrete, L., & Miller, T. (2009). A ten-year faculty mentoring program: Administrator, mentor, and mentee perspectives. *The International Journal of Learning, 16*(4), 401–415.

Tillman, L. C. (2001). Mentoring African American faculty in predominantly White institutions. *Research in Higher Education, 41*(3), 295–325.

Ulery, A. L., Sammis, T. W., & Mexal, J. G. (2004). A mentoring program that helps untenured faculty navigate the academic maze. *NACTA Journal, 48*(2), 46–51.

Vega, W., Yglesias, K., & Murray, J. P. (2010). Recruiting and mentoring minority faculty members. *New Directions for Community Colleges,* (152), 49–55. doi:10.1002/cc.427

Zachary, L. J. (2000). *The mentor's guide: Facilitating effective learning relationships.* San Francisco, CA: Jossey-Bass.

Zeind, C. S., Zdanowicz, M., MacDonald, K., Parkhurst, C., King, C., & Wizwer, P. (2005). Developing a sustainable faculty mentoring program. *American Journal of Pharmaceutical Education, 69*(5), 1–13.

Chapter 3
Professional Development Through Mentoring

Abstract Enhanced professional development occurs when faculty act as mentors for their peers, regardless of their years of seniority or stage of their career. This chapter begins with a discussion on mentoring faculty who are women and faculty from minoritized racial and ethnic groups before turning to specific ways in which colleagues may engage in mentoring to enhance professional development. Mutual benefits may be gained through mentoring that occurs in a variety of faculty relationships, including co-teaching and team teaching, reflective practice, teaching circles, and curriculum development. Each of these opportunities for mentoring will be presented in this chapter, beginning with co-teaching. Faculty who co-teach share expertise from their respective fields and in doing so learn from each other as they teach their students. Mentoring occurs in reflective practice as mentors pose thoughtful questions and ideas to engage one another in enhancing professional practice. Through teaching circles, small groups of faculty study topics related to their teaching practice, pose questions, and share ideas. Lastly, curriculum development will be described as a method for faculty to engage in mentoring to promote professional development.

Keywords Mentoring · Peer mentoring · Co-mentoring · Co-teaching · Reflective practice · Teaching circles · Curriculum development

3.1 Introduction

This chapter focuses on mentoring as professional development and professional development opportunities that encourage mentoring in higher education. Mentoring programs should be part of professional development for faculty (Buch et al. 2011). There are several reasons why mentoring promotes faculty professional development. Mentoring senior faculty has been deemed important and while it is essential for new faculty, senior faculty benefit as well (Karukstis 2010). Karukstis explained that mentoring senior faculty is important because of changing responsibilities and the invigorating results that may be achieved. Those who mentor are

D.M. Laverick, *Mentoring Processes in Higher Education*,
SpringerBriefs in Education, DOI 10.1007/978-3-319-39217-2_3

often altruistic and may also benefit through renewed interest in the field (Thurston et al. 2009). Laverick's (2005) study of expert teachers found that the teachers' professional development was enhanced in part through mentoring. This finding can translate to higher education in which teaching faculty benefit as they mentor one another.

Zachary (2000) stated that the mentor "enjoys the benefits of rich learning opportunities that mentoring provides for mentors as well as mentees. A mentor's own growth and development are nurtured through reflection, renewal, and regeneration" (p. 161). This concept is shared in the example of a veteran faculty member who explained that she has supported other faculty members by giving teaching suggestions to help them deliver their content in ways that motivate and challenge students and result in higher achievement levels of their students (Infiniti, pseudonym, personal communication, 2014). Additionally, Infiniti has supported them by providing opportunities to co-author books and articles and co-present at professional conferences.

As circumstances change and new initiatives and programs are developed, the need for mentoring at all career stages in higher education is evident. It is important to keep in mind that "good mentors must be conscious that their own professional development serves as a model" (Jonson 2008, p. 11). A faculty member who recently earned tenure, has been mentored, and now acts as a mentor shared her perspective:

> After five years, I still have to ask questions when I have a concern. I believe that mentoring takes on a different role as we progress personally and professionally. I currently have mentors that I go to when I need a listening ear, advice, compassion, a smile, a word of encouragement. Sometimes I get what I am seeking along with a re-direct, new way of thinking, conviction, and a gentle nudge. I believe we always need mentoring as we journey through our life's purpose. (Conrad, pseudonym, personal communication, 2014)

Karukstis (2010) noted that peer mentoring is one form of mentoring that would be suitable for senior faculty. "Peer mentoring is a horizontal model in which associates mentor each other" (Buch et al. 2011, p. 42). Buch and colleagues explained that peer mentoring is commonly group-based and may be formal or informal. Peer mentoring in higher education is important because "there are goals and objectives which must be met to provide students with an outstanding education" and faculty need to work together to make achieving those goals and objectives happen (Paquette, personal communication, 2014). Furthermore, Paquette elaborated that "because there are so many requirements of faculty in higher education, it is important to help each other understand those expectations."

Faculty grow professionally as a result of being a mentor. The career development needs of faculty can be addressed through a mid-career mentoring program, which begins with a needs assessment to inform the program (Buch et al. 2011). Sibert, who has been recently mentored as a new faculty member, explained that since higher education is a learning community, each person may be both a learner and a teacher through their roles as mentor and protégé. She described the mentoring process as "a circle and there are three points on the circle, which is turning clockwise. The points are mentor, mentee, and between the two is both mentor and mentee" (personal communication, 2014). This explanation illustrates how the mentor is in a position to learn from the protégé. Johnson (2007) noted the following benefits of being a mentor: "(1) personal satisfaction; (2) personal fulfillment; (3) creative synergy and professional rejuvenation; (4) networking; (5) motivation to remain current; (6) friendship and support; and (7) reputation for talent development" (pp. 12–13). Synergy is an outcome of working collaboratively with colleagues on projects, such as writing for publication (Collins et al. 2009). Collins et al. explained that the synergy that is created adds to not only the product but also the process.

Another approach to peer mentoring involves newly hired faculty mentoring one another. This relationship is different than the traditional method of having senior faculty members mentor new faculty because all participants are in the same place in their career development. Ortlieb et al. (2010) described how "newly hired faculty created a *new faculty guild* by which they would share scholarly progress, insight into effective teaching strategies, thoughts/ideas of possible research investigations, and solace for one another" (p. 109). The researchers noted that this approach to mentoring promoted a collegial environment of sharing, as opposed to competiveness, which promoted growth and advancement. One of the participants in this study explained that the members' relationship went beyond collegiality because of their simultaneously shared challenges and experiences. Ortlieb et al. offered the following suggestions for establishing new faculty communities, such as the one described in their article:

1. Schedule faculty socials near the beginning of each academic year to foster positive relationships;
2. Encourage joint research and publication ventures;
3. Encourage new faculty to seek out a network of others with similar interests, including senior faculty, newly hired faculty, and professionals from the field of study;
4. Offer monthly discussions over lunch where faculty can present their current research so as to offer direction, guidance, and opportunities for collaboration; and
5. Prompt new faculty to critically reflect and adjust accordingly to bridge the transition from student to faculty member (p. 116).

Kawalilak and Groen (2010) described their experiences as two female faculty who were working toward earning tenure. Their experience of mentoring each other resembles the idea presented by Ortlieb et al. with regard to new faculty mentoring each other, without the community-approach described by Ortlieb et al. Rather, Kawalilak and Groen focused on the power of co-mentoring each other as they pursued tenure. In addition to co-mentoring, they sought mentors in senior faculty and those in leadership positions to share their knowledge and experiences. Kawalilak and Groen advised that having more faculty resources of support would be beneficial. They stated, "Although we offered support and insight to one another, were we not the blind leading the blind? Extending our network of support would ensure a more critical perspective and understanding of our experiences as novice faculty" (p. 140).

The assignment of mentors, even in the case of peer mentoring, needs to be carefully considered. For peer mentoring to be effective, it is essential that the mentors are able to provide what each other needs. In a case study published by Frazier (2011), a participant who was a new faculty member was assigned a mentor who also did not have tenure. She shared this example to illustrate how a department chair assigned a mentor who, since she had not been tenured herself, limited the participant's ability to earn tenure.

3.2 Mentoring Faculty that Include Women and Minoritized Racial and Ethnic Groups

Female faculty members or those who are from minoritized racial and ethnic groups have unique needs that may be met through peer mentoring. This section will discuss first the mentoring needs of female faculty before turning toward the needs of those from minoritized racial and ethnic groups.

3.2.1 Mentoring Faculty Who Are Women

A study of academic women faculty found that just over half had a current mentor but yet most desired mentoring (Blood et al. 2012). These researchers identified gaps in mentoring that varied according to rank, research focus, parenting, and work time status. For example, the study found that assistant professors were more likely to need mentoring related to scholarship whereas the needs of associate professors related to program development. Furthermore, the study indicated that faculty who are parents need mentoring related to balancing work with family life. Blood and colleagues' study concluded:

> Recognizing that these issues are likely to evolve as a faculty member progresses through her career is critical. Addressing these needs and gaps by taking into account developmental and situational stages in careers and training mentors to ask specifically about these areas has the potential to create more successful frameworks for structuring mentoring initiatives. (p. 1207)

To illustrate the unique mentoring needs of female faculty, a junior faculty member explained that as a female, she felt that she wanted to "feel welcomed and cared about, maybe more so or in a different way that a man would" (Sibert, personal communication, 2014). She also believed that if you are working in an environment of mostly women, there are unique issues that arise. This concept aligns with the work of Thurston et al. (2009) who advised that the needs of protégés differ not only from year to year but also from mentee to mentee.

A horizontal peer mentoring approach was successful in promoting the career development of senior women chemists at liberal arts colleges (Karukstis 2010). Karukstis reported that the participants shared ideas, experiences, and expertise; articulated short-term and long-term career goals; and formulated action plans to attain these goals. Another outcome of this project, according to Karukstis, was the impact that it made on the participants' undergraduate research programs.

Buch et al. (2011) sought "to design a faculty-development program that would facilitate the promotion of associate professors to the rank of full professor" and administered a needs assessment to the intended participants (p. 40). Buch and her colleagues "identified some dramatic gender differences that may help to explain the phenomenon of more women than men standing still at associate" professor rank (p. 41). A significant amount of female participants in this study (73 %) perceived that challenges faced by associate professors prevented or delayed their promotion as compared to 51 % of male participants. Other significant findings of Buch et al.'s study revealed that the female participants were more likely to disagree with statements regarding: the clear criteria for deciding promotion to full professor; receiving guidance from the department chairperson on what was needed for promotion; and the belief that decisions about promotion to full professor were fair and not influenced by gender, race, or other non-performance factors. The researchers administered a second survey two years after a mid-career mentoring program was developed. The results of the second survey revealed that more women participated in the mentoring initiatives and there was "a significant reduction in the gender gap that was revealed in the first survey" (p. 44). The female participants "still perceived more barriers to promotion and a greater need for policy changes to remove those barriers than men" but yet some of the items to which they responded revealed no significant gender differences.

3.2.2 Mentoring Faculty from Minoritized Racial and Ethnic Groups

Regardless of the stage of one's career in higher education, mentoring for faculty from minoritized racial and ethnic groups is critical. As one faculty member shared,

> I believe that as humankind, we feel most comfortable in the company of those that we feel an ethnic, cultural, language connection. I often think about being the only African American in many meetings, and professional roles, where some people may not be as comfortable with me as I am with them, because I have always been the minority and am accustomed to adjusting to environments where there are few if any other minorities. (Conrad, pseudonym, personal communication, 2014)

Similarly, Evans and Packer-Williams (2011) stated, "Women and minorities, in general, may feel uncomfortable with the concept of being groomed or cloned fearing they must give up their identities" (para 2). Effective mentoring helps to address this concern. Cohen and Galbraith (1995) explained that "important influences on the mentoring relationship, such as ethnicity, age, and socioeconomic background can be approached from several perspectives" (p. 13). These perspectives, according to Cohen and Galbraith, include the "recognition that people contain a multitude of legitimate, positive, and exciting differences is an intrinsically valuable part of the learning experience" (p. 13) and that the "mentoring relationship offers an opportunity for both mentors and mentees to learn how to explore real-world differences between them, differences that often are not obvious" (p. 13).

Evans and Packer-Williams (2011) studied the participation of new African American female faculty members' participation in a peer mentoring group. These authors stated that peer mentoring is important for retaining faculty of color; additionally, African American women were able to identify and access other African American women in their workplace in which discrimination and oppression were minimized. Evans and Packer-Williams stated that the peer mentoring group, which was comprised of five newly hired African American female professors, had three main goals:

> (a) to assist each other in scholarly efforts through collaborative research publications and presentations, (b) to provide opportunities for members to voice their concerns and have them validated by other African American women in the academy, and (c) to combat the isolation in the academy by participating in social events together held inside and outside of the university setting. (para 14)

The results of Evans and Packer-Williams' study found three themes related to the impact that peer mentoring made on the participants: "(a) peer mentoring as a vehicle to process and cope effectively with microaggressions, (b) peer mentoring as a strategy to increase positive self-identity and self-efficacy as a scholar, and (c) peer mentoring as an approach to recognizing and combating internalized oppression and stereotypes" (para 19). Furthermore, the authors noted that the results of this study point toward the benefit of group peer mentoring on faculty productivity.

One of the challenges of mentoring faculty members from minoritized racial and ethnic groups is finding mentors who are able to best meet their needs. For example, Frazier (2011) stated that there is a lack of African American senior faculty members, which leads to pairing African American faculty members with non-African American faculty members. She explained that Black faculty may experience difficulty, therefore having a mentor with whom they may share their feelings of isolation, acts of racism, and microaggressions is helpful. Furthermore, she stated that it is difficult for African American faculty to find mentors within their department and institution with similar interests.

3.3 Co-teaching and Team Teaching

Co-teaching and team teaching in higher education provide an opportunity for mentoring to occur as faculty collaboratively teach a course. While co-teaching and team teaching are different approaches to teaching, the concept of having two faculty members collaborate to teach a course and be present together in the same classroom is the premise of this chapter on peer mentoring. Co-teaching involves two credentialed professionals who offer joint delivery of instruction to a diverse group of students within a shared classroom space (Friend and Cook 2010). In higher education, co-teaching may be used as an instructional model for preservice teachers to prepare them for this approach to teaching that takes place in K-12 classrooms.

One example of team teaching as a form of mentoring involves a junior faculty member who team teaches a graduate course with a senior faculty member. The junior faculty member explained that she observes how the experienced faculty member handles the course; she listens and watches in order to inform her procedures and practice (Sibert, personal communication, 2014). The junior faculty member was able to gain insight into the preparation, planning, instruction, and assessment procedures that are associated with teaching a graduate level course. Furthermore, because this particular course is taught at campus different from the main campus, the faculty partners had travel time to and from their teaching assignment. The faculty members had an extended opportunity for collaboration and time to debrief while traveling to and from class. Figure 3.1 shows Dr. DeAnna Laverick and Dr. George Bieger as they collaborated prior to the start of their team-taught class.

While these faculty members from the team teaching example were from the same department and had similar backgrounds of experience, similar benefits are attained when faculty from different departments co-teach courses. For example, co-taught courses for early childhood/special education dual certification majors

Fig. 3.1 Dr. DeAnna Laverick and Dr. George Bieger engaged in peer mentoring while team teaching a graduate education course. *Photo credit* Kimberly Mohney

provide peer mentoring opportunities for faculty from each of these disciplines as they learn from each other through co-teaching. While the faculty may have the same years of experience and/or rank, their content knowledge is something that may be shared through this type of mentoring relationship. Furthermore, each person brings different content knowledge and skill sets to the teaching situation based on their own unique experiences and academic preparation. This arrangement also facilitates collaboration on scholarly projects as each person provides a different perspective on a topic based on his or her field of expertise.

3.4 Reflective Practice and Teaching Circles

Reflective practice engages faculty in thoughtful consideration of their teaching and mentors serve as a resource for protégés who have questions that stem from reflective practice. Danielson (1996) described reflection upon teaching as the "mark of a true professional" (p. 106) and through reflection, growth and excellence are possible. She defined reflection as "the thinking that follows any instructional event" (p. 106). Sternberg (2001) explained that "experts need to develop a sense of their own efficacy to solve difficult tasks in their domain of expertise" (p. 164). To be aware of their own level of efficacy, teachers need to engage in reflective practice. With regard to mentoring, mentors have the ability to extend protégés' professional development by sharing wisdom and expertise and by asking questions to engage the protégé in becoming a reflective practitioner. Being a mentor provides an opportunity for faculty to engage in reflective practice.

> In working with a mentee, the mentor is forced to reflect on his own practice, choices, and beliefs! Life doesn't allow much time for this otherwise, but when you are in the mentoring role, you have no choice but to reflect, which I know to be one of the most important paths to professional improvement. (Sibert, personal communication, 2014)

Similar to Sibert's expression of difficulty finding time to reflect, encouraging reflective thought was identified by Ghosh (2013) as a challenging function performed by mentors. Danielson (1996) noted that differences exist in how novice and experienced teachers reflect on the effectiveness of a lesson. Teachers who are characterized by their expertise are articulate about their work, being able to explain both what they did during their teaching practices and why (Mosenthal et al. 2004). Regardless of a faculty member's years of seniority, the instructor could move into a novice role if assigned to teach a new course or perform a new job-related task. In this type of situation, mentoring can assist faculty in becoming proficient at the new task or assignment and help colleagues move into what Danielson refers to as the 'distinguished' level of performance. Reflection is a metacognitive process that is a characteristic of expertise (Sternberg 2001) and a professional responsibility described by existing literature (Danielson 1996; Morrow and Asbury 2003; Mosenthal et al. 2004). In peer mentoring, colleagues may support each other to become metacognitive about their teaching by engaging in reflection.

Another way that senior faculty may be mentored is through professional development experiences provided by other faculty. At Indiana University of Pennsylvania, the Center for Teaching Excellence supports faculty by organizing presentations, large-group reflective practice opportunities, and teaching circles, which are small groups of faculty who are engaged in reflective practice based on a topic of interest to group members. As a former board member of the Center for Teaching Excellence, Dr. Valeri Helterbran gave presentations to faculty who participated in the reflective practice program on various aspects of pedagogy and scholarship (personal communication, 2014). Ford (pseudonym, personal communication, 2014) explained that she participates in reflective practice and believes that in her department it is focused on helping new faculty. She suggested that programs such as reflective practice should include workshops on what it takes to be a good mentor. As such, organized presentations such as those given by Helterbran provide opportunities for mentoring.

Caution should be used when mentors are placed in a situation in which they observe protégés and are required to evaluate their teaching. A study conducted by Ingleby (2014) found that participants in a mentoring program valued the emphasis placed on reflective practice but yet a concern was expressed regarding the need to observe and assess the protégés' teaching. Based on the findings of this study, Ingleby concluded that a goal of mentor training should be reflective practice and protégés' teaching should be supported in a developmental manner rather than through a judgmental model. The concern regarding assessing protégés' teaching relates to an approach that utilizes observation and reflection, Japanese Lesson Study, which is discussed next.

3.4.1 *Japanese Lesson Study as a Method of Mentoring*

Japanese Lesson Study is a teaching technique that is centered on reflection and may be used in higher education to facilitate mentoring. Roback et al. (2006) defined Japanese Lesson Study as "a collaborative approach for teachers to plan, present, observe, and critique classroom lessons. Through the lesson study process, teachers systematically and thoughtfully examine both student learning and their own teaching practices" (para 1). These authors used Japanese Lesson Study in an upper-level undergraduate statistics course. In a mentoring relationship, the use of Japanese Lesson Study has the potential to support faculty members in refining their teaching skills through collaborative planning, observation, and reflection. While senior faculty who are mentoring new faculty might find this technique highly useful, the technique would serve in peer mentoring situations among all faculty, regardless of rank or tenure status.

The benefits of Japanese Lesson Study in higher education were described by Roback et al. (2006) as: focused and energized collaboration, insight into student learning, development of a strong lesson plan, and facilitation of pedagogical research.

Burghes and Robinson (2009) described the use of Japanese Lesson Study with groups of teachers at the school and college levels according to the following stages:

1. "Choose a research theme: a group of teachers agree a [*sic*] research theme, often school/college-wide and involving student skills or attitudes that the school or college wishes to promote;
2. focus the research: the group chooses a unit of study to focus on and considers the overall research theme in this context;
3. create the lesson: the group selects a lesson or lessons within the unit to concentrate on, using a lesson planning template to plan lessons jointly;
4. teach and observe the lesson: the lesson is taught by a member of the group and observed by the other members; the focus of the observation is on student thinking and responses rather than the teacher's ability;
5. discuss the lesson: the group gets together, usually on the day of the lesson, to discuss the outcomes of the lesson and their observations;
6. revise the lesson: revisions are made to the lesson, based on the observations and one of the group is selected to teach the lesson again; the cycle of observation, discussion and revision is repeated if necessary;
7. document the findings: at the end of this process, the group produces a report that outlines what they have learnt with regard to the research theme and goal;
8. present the findings: the group presents its findings to other groups and/or conferences. The length of the process varies but it is not uncommon to take up to a year or two. The size of the group also varies but typically involves four to six teachers, as well as an administrator and external expert. The whole process is thought of as a bridge formed by teachers working together and collaborating across the curriculum rather than in isolation". (p. 7)

Following these steps promotes enhanced teaching through mentoring that occurs in lesson study. The observation, reflection, and dialogue that take place in this approach serve as a springboard to critical inquiry into improving professional practice through the support of mentors.

3.5 Mentoring Through Curriculum Development

Curriculum development is an area where mentorship needs to occur, especially as faculty of differing levels of experience collaborate to write new curriculum and revise existing curriculum. Creative mentorship experiences may also be built into the curriculum. For example, as co-taught courses are being proposed, this form of mentoring becomes integrated into curriculum development. One way in which this integration occurs is through writing the course description, objectives, assessments, calendar, etc. As faculty collaborate to develop courses, in this case a co-taught course, the need to plan for the roles that each faculty member plays is crucial. Considerations such as the timing, model of co-teaching being used, materials, etc. have to be discussed. Within this situation, mentoring occurs and this mentoring opportunity leads to professional growth for the faculty involved.

In general, senior faculty are in an influential position to mentor junior faculty in the curriculum development process. This process is important because of the impact it makes on content delivery and student achievement. Ford shared that she has co-written curriculum with a new faculty member who expressed a desire to learn how the curriculum process works (pseudonym, personal communication, 2014). When teams of faculty work together to collaboratively propose and revise curriculum, opportunities for mentoring occur. Mutual benefits are gained as different ideas, perspectives, backgrounds, and experiences are shared.

References

Blood, E. A., Ullrich, M. D., Hirshfeld-Becker, D. R., Seely, E. W., Connelly, M. T., Warfield, C. A., & Emans, S. J. (2012). Academic women faculty: Are they finding the mentoring they need? *Journal of Women's Health, 21*(11), 1201–1208. doi:10.1089/jwh.2012.3529

Buch, K., Huet, Y., Rorrer, A., & Roberson, L. (2011). Removing the barriers to full professor: A mentoring program for associate professors. *The Magazine for Higher Learning, 43*(6), 38–45.

Burghes, D., & Robinson, D. (2009). Lesson study: Enhancing mathematics teaching and learning. Reading, Berkshire, United Kingdom: CfBT Education Trust. Retrieved from http://www.cimt.plymouth.ac.uk/papers/lessonstudy.pdf

Cohen, N. H., & Galbraith, M. W. (1995). Mentoring in the learning society. In M. W. Galbraith & N. H. Cohen (Eds.), *Mentoring: New strategies and challenges* (pp. 5–14). San Francisco, CA: Jossey-Bass.

Collins, T., Slough, S., & Waxman, H. (2009). Lessons learned about mentoring junior faculty in higher education. *Academic Leadership, 7*(2), 18–22.

Danielson, C. (1996). *Enhancing professional practice: A framework for teaching*. Alexandria, VA: Association for Supervision and Curriculum Development.

Evans, K. M., & Packer-Williams, C. L. (2011). Retaining and reclaiming ourselves: Reflections on a peer mentoring group experience for new African American women professors. *Perspectives in Peer Programs, 23*(1), 9–23.

Frazier, K. N. (2011). Academic bullying: A barrier to tenure and promotion for African-American faculty. *Florida Journal of Educational Administration & Policy, 5*(1), 1–13.

Friend, M., & Cook, L. (2010). *Interactions: Collaboration skills for school professionals*. Boston: Pearson.

Ghosh, R. (2013). Mentors providing challenge and support: Integrating concepts from teacher mentoring in education and organizational mentoring in business. Human Resource Development Review, *12*(2), 144–176. doi:10.1177/1534484312465608

Ingleby, E. (2014). Developing reflective practice or judging teaching performance? The implications for mentor training. *Research in Post-Compulsory Education, 19*(1), 18–32. doi:10.1080/13596748.2014.872917

Johnson, W. B. (2007). *On being a mentor: A guide for higher education faculty*. Mahwah, NJ: Lawrence Erlbaum Associates.

Jonson, K. F. (2008). Passing the torch. In C. Press (Ed.), *Mentoring, coaching, and collaboration* (pp. 1–11). Thousand Oaks, CA: Sage.

Karukstis, K. K. (2010). Horizontal mentoring initiative for senior women scientists at liberal arts colleges. *Council on Undergraduate Research Quarterly, 31*(2), 33–39.

Kawalilak, C., & Groen, J. (2010). Illuminating the tenure-track pathway: A "new" faculty perspective. *Journal of Educational Thought, 44*(1), 131–146.

Laverick, D. M. (2005). *A qualitative study of teachers certified by the National Board for Professional Teaching Standards and their expertise in promoting early literacy.* Retrieved from Proquest Information and Learning Company. (UMI Microform 3165958).

Morrow, L. M., & Asbury, E. (2003). Current practices in early literacy development. In L. M. Morrow, L. B. Gambrell, & M. Pressley (Eds.), *Best practices in literacy instruction* (2nd ed., pp. 43–63). New York: Guilford Press.

Mosenthal, J., Lipson, M., Torncello, S., Russ, B., & Mekkelsen, J. (2004). Contexts and practices of six schools successful in obtaining reading achievement. *The Elementary School Journal, 104*(5), 343–367.

Ortlieb, E. T., Biddix, J. P., & Doepker, G. M. (2010). A collaborative approach to higher education induction. *Active Learning in Higher Education, 11*(2), 109–118. doi:10.1177/1469787410365655

Roback, P., Chance, B., Legler, J., & Moore, T. (2006). Applying Japanese lesson study principles to an upper-level undergraduate statistics course. *Journal of Statistics Education, 14*(2). Retrieved from http://www.amstat.org/publications/jse/v14n2/roback.html

Sternberg, R. J. (2001). Giftedness as developing expertise: A theory of the interface between high abilities and achieved excellence. *High Ability Studies, 12*(2), 159–178.

Thurston, L. P., Navarrete, L., & Miller, T. (2009). A ten-year faculty mentoring program: Administrator, mentor, and mentee perspectives. *The International Journal of Learning, 16*(4), 401–415.

Zachary, L. J. (2000). *The mentor's guide: Facilitating effective learning relationships*. San Francisco, CA: Jossey-Bass.

Chapter 4
Mentoring Graduate Students

Abstract The mentoring relationship between faculty and graduate students is unique and mutually beneficial. In some circumstances, graduate students may be working as they take graduate classes and their careers may be a source for collaborative research projects. By establishing mentoring partnerships with graduate students, faculty stay close to the "trenches" in their fields and have a practical understanding of the realities that their students face in their careers. Students who are mentored by faculty gain expertise in their field as they learn current research and study the theories that inform their practice. Students who work as research assistants and teaching associates at the university level learn from their mentors as they observe their mentors' work and pattern their practice after their mentors. As such, the role of the faculty mentor is critical when working with graduate students because they are shaping the future of the profession. This chapter will describe how graduate students are mentored through scholarly projects and internships before turning toward a description of the unique needs of mentoring graduate students who are women and those from minoritized racial and ethnic groups.

Keywords Mentoring · Mentoring graduate students · Mentoring through research · Mentoring through internships · Mentoring female graduate students · Mentoring graduate students from minoritized groups

4.1 Introduction

Mentoring opportunities abound for faculty who work with graduate students. In addition to teaching graduate students, faculty may chair and serve on dissertation committees, supervise graduate and/or teaching assistants, and collaborate on scholarly projects with graduate students who have similar interests. Helterbran explained that faculty are a part of all who we have met; therefore, we learn and grow from our students in a multitude of ways (personal communication, 2014). Figure 4.1 shows Dr. Valeri Helterbran, who mentored her graduate student, Kris Glosser.

D.M. Laverick, *Mentoring Processes in Higher Education*,
SpringerBriefs in Education, DOI 10.1007/978-3-319-39217-2_4

Fig. 4.1 Dr. Valeri Helterbran mentoring her graduate student, Kris Glosser. *Photo credit* Dr. Valeri Helterbran

Lechuga (2011) studied the perceptions of faculty advisors' perceived roles and relationships with graduate students. Lechuga found the following themes, which characterize these roles and responsibilities: (1) Faculty as Advisor (i.e., providing academic advice and personal support); (2) Faculty as Instructor (i.e., helping graduate students develop certain skills in formal learning situations); (3) Faculty as Employer (i.e., acting in the role of a supervisor toward a staff member); and (4) Faculty as Agent of Socialization (i.e., developing professional skills and initiating the graduate students into the norms and values of their disciplines). Lechuga described the relationship components studied as being fluid in nature rather than compartmentalized behaviors.

An important consideration for mentoring graduate students relates to the experience of the faculty member. Lechuga (2011) found differences in the ways in which graduate students were mentored according to the faculty mentor's status as either nontenured or tenured faculty. For example, Lechuga noted that nontenured faculty expected the graduate students to work independently, have high computational and mathematical skills, and take initiative. Tenured faculty, according to Lechuga, had similar expectations but also focused on having their graduate students make conference presentations and engage in networking and also helped them relate to other scholars in non-academic ways. With these findings in mind, a goal of all faculty should be to help graduate students grow as scholars and therefore, support them by including them in their mentors' scholarly endeavors. This chapter shares ways in which graduate students learn about the workings of higher education (beyond being a student) through effective mentoring.

Mentoring graduate students involves more than just teaching, according to Lea (2011), who explained,

> Teaching and mentoring are not mutually inclusive as students are not always mentees to mentors. Mentoring is one form of teaching; however, teaching in the classroom, advising the program sequence, or dissertation advising is doubtfully qualified automatically to be mentoring. (p. 261)

Lea continued by stating that mentoring is more expansive and substantial than teaching and advising and "is marked by intellectual connection and an empowering influence. The connection intimates the level of trust and the degree of academic influence that the mentee and the mentor reciprocate" (p. 263).

Graduate students are in a special position to become immersed in the culture of higher education. Mentoring in this capacity functions as supervision for assisting graduate students who are teaching and also provides graduate students with a repertoire of helpful ideas or guidance. One mentor for graduate students advised that it is important to spend time with graduate students and really listen (Paquette, personal communication, 2014). Furthermore, she provides resources and examples for them to follow, when possible.

Jiang stated that "mentoring in higher education is necessary because it helps students better prepare for their future work and professional development" (personal communication, 2014). Graduate assistants and teaching associates are often fully immersed in the teaching, scholarship, and perhaps service components that comprise the professional responsibilities of faculty. A doctoral candidate who is also a graduate assistant (GA) shared:

> Mentoring allows for positive interactions, which are the cornerstone of experiences. Higher education can be challenging and the guidance, support, and mentoring allow for a feeling of 'I'm not alone' and self-confidence to begin to grow. It allows GAs and students to feel a sense of pride and connectedness in their work and higher education. It also allows for the ability to see ourselves progressing in higher education. (Casses, personal communication, 2014)

As teaching associates, graduate students benefit from having a faculty mentor to provide them with feedback on their teaching, scholarship, and other responsibilities. Feedback on lessons observed by faculty mentors helps improve teaching. For example, one teaching associate shared that his mentor observed and recommended that he use other techniques beyond lecture to engage the undergraduate students he taught. He adjusted his instruction based on this recommendation, which improved student engagement in his classes (Wen, personal communication, 2014).

It is important for mentors to make their graduate student protégés feel welcome to approach them with concerns. Jiang stated, "My mentor is a very nice person. She is encouraging and supportive so I was not afraid of asking her questions regarding work and study. Having my questions answered helped me better finish my work and better face challenges" (personal communication, 2014).

Collaboration provides an opportunity for mentors and protégés to each bring something to the mentoring relationship. As stated by Helterbran, "Mentoring is not a one way street" (personal communication, 2014). A graduate student offered this perspective on collaborating with her faculty mentor, "We meet on a regular basis so my mentor and I can share a lot of ideas on study and work. My feedback helps her to better understand students' needs and sometimes give her inspirations on her research" (Jiang, personal communication, 2014). This idea of a mutually beneficial relationship is evident in the relationship that Casses has with her mentor. She stated:

> I think that another important aspect of mentoring is the ability of the mentor to treat the student as an equal who is in a different stage of the growth process... she treats me as an equal (even though I'm not) and she doesn't put herself on a pedestal (even though she should). I think that is what makes her so very special to me. I find that there is a comfort with her that also encourages me to always do my best work FOR her... It's like she remembers that she was where I am at one time and empathizes with that. (personal communication, 2014)

This quote illustrates the importance of how a mentor approaches the mentoring relationship by recognizing that each person is at a different stage of his or her professional development but yet brings valuable experience to the shared, common experience. This quote also underscores the protégé's view that the quality of her work is important so that she upholds the ideals that are important to both parties in this relationship. Furthermore, the concept of mentors treating their graduate student protégés as equals was verified in the research conducted by Nakamura et al. (2009) who stated,

> Effective mentors treated students as equal collaborators, helped students secure funding during graduate study (and sometimes a desirable position afterward), offered encouragement, provided counsel as necessary, showed their humanness and vulnerabilities by related personal struggles similar to those of students, and assessed what was going well with students' work as well as what could be improved. (p. 248)

In addition to establishing positive mentoring relationships between graduate students and their advisors, it is necessary to maintain these relationships. A study conducted by Mansson and Myers (2012) examined the relational maintenance behaviors that advisees used to maintain these relationships. These researchers identified six relational maintenance behaviors: appreciation, tasks, protection, courtesy, humor, and goals and these behaviors provide a framework from which advisees may work to sustain positive relationships with their advisors. Furthermore, Mansson and Myers found that when advisees are appreciative, courteous, humorous, protect their advisors' reputation, complete assigned tasks, and discuss their goals, advisors provide them with career and psychosocial support.

A study conducted by Miller and Deggs (2012) replicated a study of mentoring graduate students through graduate student organizations that was completed by Miller and Dirkx in 1995. In comparing contemporary mentoring programs with the programs in the initial study, Miller and Deggs found that contemporary programs were much less focused on professional socialization and mentoring and seemed to be doing less than in the previous study. These authors explained that perhaps the reason for this finding was due to graduate students being spread out among different sites, rather than being housed in one residential location. Furthermore, the authors also attributed the decline to multiple academic programs being housed together administratively in a multidiscipline format. The authors also speculated that a cause for the decline may be due to limited resources or a work environment that may have changed to promote individual rather than collective rewards and activities. The implications of this study, according to Miller and Deggs, relate to the possible extinction of graduate student organizations, attention to determining the online mentoring of graduate students, and the need for faculty to model the social integration that they seek to develop in their students.

4.2 Mentoring Through Scholarly Projects

Faculty have an opportunity to mentor graduate students as they collaborate on scholarly activities. For example, they may work together to prepare professional presentations, co-author publications, or engage in distance technologies to guide and shape students' dissertations (Helterbran, personal communication, 2014). To elaborate,

> For students interested in careers in academe, there is simply no substitute for being trained and mentored by a productive sponsor and collaborating with one's sponsor during graduate school. Outstanding mentors understand this benefit and often go to great lengths to find ways to appropriately incorporate novice protégés into ongoing scholarly projects. (Johnson 2007, p. 8)

A doctoral candidate described how a faculty mentor had a firm but caring approach toward her as she engaged in research (Casses, personal communication, 2014). She elaborated by sharing that this particular mentor had a high standard that she will always strive to maintain, in terms of accountability and academic output. Zachary (2000) advised that there are three critical aspects of accountability:

1. Ground rules, which are the norms or accepted behaviors
2. Confidentiality, which entails clarification of what confidentiality and consensus mean
3. Boundary setting, which involves the mentor and the protégé setting boundaries so that limits are not exceeded and negatively impact the relationship

As a graduate assistant, the opportunities to engage in scholarly activities are numerous. One graduate assistant described her experience:

> ...being present in the day-to-day [activities] of the University allows for more opportunities to meet faculty and find one's own way in higher education–getting to know different professors and then finding your own "self" while observing others allows for getting to know and being mentored by different individuals within different stages, projects, and needs. (Casses, personal communication, 2014)

A graduate student shared her belief that positive mentoring relationships rely on the mentor. If a mentor is willing to be dedicated to a mentoring relationship, it means that he or she cares about the students' needs, supports them in different ways, values their feedback and tries to keep them closely connected (Jiang, personal communication, 2014). Nakamura et al. (2009) provided the following recommendations for mentors:

- "Know yourself" (p. 253).
- "Work with young people who are a good match" (p. 254).
- "Address individual differences" (p. 254).
- "Enact key values and practices in plain view" (p. 255).
- "Think out loud" (p. 255).
- "Create a community that complements and amplifies the direct transmission of knowledge, values, and practices" (p. 255).
- "Help students learn by doing" (p. 256).
- "Facilitate students' building of social capital" (p. 256).

For protégés, Nakamura et al. (2009) recommended the following:

- "Know yourself" (p. 257).
- "Seek a good fit in a mentor" (p. 258).
- "Seek a good fit in a learning and working environment" (p. 258).
- "Play an active role in learning from others" (p. 259).
- "Seek out multiple influences" (p. 259).

Last, Nakamura et al. (2009) offered the following recommendations for institutions:

- "Support mentoring" (p. 260).
- "Reward mentoring" (p. 261).
- "Prepare future mentors" (p. 261).

Taken collectively, the research conducted by Nakamura and colleagues offers key guidelines for building effective mentoring relationships in higher education.

An opportunity exists in a three-way mentoring partnership in supervising doctoral dissertations. Collins et al. (2009) advised that new faculty co-chair doctoral dissertations with experienced senior faculty in order to learn the dissertation process from the faculty member's perspective. In this way, two faculty members are providing mentorship to a graduate student but yet a junior faculty member is also being mentored by a senior faculty member. Beyond scholarly projects, internships and teaching experiences provide other avenues through which graduate students may grow as professionals in the areas of professional interests shared with faculty mentors. This topic is discussed in the next section.

4.3 Mentoring Though Internships and Teaching

Mentoring through internships provide enriching experiences for graduate students because of the opportunity that is presented to work directly with faculty or professional supervisors. For example, a veteran faculty member who was a former principal, mentors principal and doctoral interns (Infiniti, pseudonym, personal communication, 2014). This faculty member, based on her experience, provided an excellent model for her interns. Nakamura et al. (2009) found that "talk and direct dialogue was a less salient means of transmitting values and practices… modeling appeared to be a more powerful mode of influence" (pp. 240–241). As an example of one doctoral candidate's mentoring experience during a college-teaching type of internship, she described the impact that her mentor made through modeling:

> She carefully and skillfully taught me the art of teaching through her own modeling, feedback, and support. Her guidance encouraged me to be 'me' while teaching–and her grounded and down-to-earth persona practices what she preaches. I have been truly blessed to have had, and continue to have, her mentorship. (Casses, personal communication, 2014)

This example aligns with the idea of mentor as model described by Daloz (1999), "Mentors most obviously provide vision by modeling the person whom the protégé wants to become" (p. 223). Zachary (2000) cautioned that mentors must differentiate between self and other in order to avoid cloning, or projecting their own lived experience onto the protégé. By allowing the protégé to be herself while teaching, the mentor is what Daloz describes as holding up a mirror to help the student develop self-awareness. Nakamura et al. (2009) suggested that an ideal situation would be for mentors to use modeling and conversation because these modes provide mutual reinforcement. According to Cohen and Galbraith (1995), internship instructors dramatically influence the learner as a new practitioner through ongoing dialogues and hands-on demonstrations. They elaborated by sharing that internship instructors who are mentors, "provide enriched learning opportunities and enable their adult learners to benefit from all the potential offered by the internship model" (p. 9). In this fashion, Paquette stated that she provides graduate students with the opportunity to observe her teaching, and then if they are interested, they are able to teach while she stays in the classroom, observes, and gives feedback (personal communication, 2014). In another internship example, Casses stated that her mentor allowed her to embrace the process of managing stress at a high level (personal communication, 2014). She further explained that her mentor's constant emotional and academic encouragement allowed her "confidence to remain steady and grounded through a time of intense stress." The need for faculty mentors to support graduate students both academically and emotionally is supported by research conducted by Lechuga (2011).

Stress is an overall challenge that graduate students can learn to manage through mentoring. Relatedly, graduate students face a challenge in learning time management and strategies for balancing responsibilities that relate to work, projects, and personal responsibilities. Heider explained that the biggest challenge she faced was juggling work, school, and family while working toward earning her doctoral degree. She shared that the advice and support of professors and cohort members was invaluable as she struggled to keep everything in balance (personal communication, 2014).

Mentors may support graduate students who serve as graduate or teaching assistants by setting realistic expectations and goals, and providing additional clarification as needed as opposed to letting them figure it out on their own (Murray, personal communication, 2014). Additionally, Murray explained that her mentor assigned projects that were meaningful and therefore contributed to her growth as a doctoral candidate.

4.4 Mentoring Graduate Students that Include Women and Minoritized Racial and Ethnic Groups

Female graduate students or those who are from minoritized racial and ethnic groups have unique needs that may be met through mentoring. This section will discuss first the mentoring needs of female graduate students before turning toward the needs of those from minoritized racial and ethnic groups.

4.4.1 Mentoring Graduate Students Who Are Women

Being a female graduate student presents unique challenges that mentors have the potential to help their mentees overcome. For example, a doctoral candidate noted that "mentoring took on a role of support not only in the realm of higher education, but the management of life while pursuing my doctorate. The process of pursuing a doctorate with children, a husband, and life can seem insurmountable at times" (Casses, personal communication, 2014). In this particular situation, having a mentor who experienced the same types of challenges is helpful. Specifically, Heider advised that it would be helpful for women to have female mentors because she believes:

> Women have greater challenges than men when it comes to pursuing a degree in higher education. Because women are typically the primary caregivers of children, as well as the primary custodians of the home, and many of them also work outside the home, they must develop excellent time management skills as they struggle to balance work, school, and family. I think it helps if women are mentored by other women who have been able to successfully balance work, school, and family while attaining a degree. (personal communication, 2014)

In other words, the mentor is a role model who can advise the protégé on strategies for overcoming the similar obstacles that were faced. As one graduate student explained,

> I think as women, and especially mothers in the field of education, we are managing heavy loads and multiple hats as we progress through intensive studies. Not to downplay the roles of men, but to recognize that women are wired in different ways. The emotional needs of women are typically greater and more active than men, so I feel that support from a relational level is essential in the process. I know from my own experience that this is what has gotten me through to this point. (Casses, personal communication, 2014)

4.4.2 Mentoring Graduate Students from Minoritized Racial and Ethnic Groups

Lechuga (2011) found differences between the ways in which faculty mentors mentored graduate students of different races/ethnicities. Lechuga explained a difference as being:

> The degree of self-efficacy, especially in the Latino students, was much lower when compared to domestic White males. As such, Latino faculty participants spent additional time mentoring Latino students in ways to increase their confidence in their abilities to succeed in academic endeavors. (p. 762)

One of the findings of Evans and Packer-Williams' (2011) study of African American women who were new faculty participating in a peer mentoring group included the participants' lack of a strong and positive self-identify and self-efficacy. The authors attributed this finding to a lack of mentoring in the participants' doctoral studies and entrance into their role as new faculty. Evans and Packer-Williams' shared a quote by one of the participants:

> In my doctoral program, I did not have the type of mentoring that I really needed to be successful in the academy. In other words, I did not have professors who were willing to take me under their wing and show me the ropes… Now I realize the importance of having someone to guide your way, answer your questions, teach you about departmental politics and include you on research projects for authorship as a new faculty member. (para 23)

This study's findings point to the importance of providing effective mentoring to support the needs of graduate students from minoritized racial and ethnic groups.

Another consideration relates to the difference in perception of race between the mentor and the protégé. Barker's (2011) study revealed that many of the Black doctoral students in his study perceived their race to be a liability, while their advisors viewed race as leverage for being sought after for jobs. Similarly, perceptions of efficacy may differ between graduate student instructors and the students they teach. A graduate student who served as a teaching associate took the advice of his mentor to be confident in teaching and hold firm to standards to overcome a challenge that he felt was a result of being a graduate student instructor who was also from a minoritized racial group (Wen, personal communication, 2014). Wen explained that he needed to "establish authority and trust among students, especially when just starting to teach new groups of students." The advice of the faculty advisor in this situation aligns with the recommendation made by Barker (2011) that "in order to promote positive cross-race interactions… it is extremely important for faculty and students, particularly those who operate in racially complicated contexts, to have a shared understanding of the racial and cultural history of their context" (p. 392).

A study that investigated the impact of race had on the advising relationship between Black doctoral students and their advisors found that White faculty can be effective advisors in cross-race relationships (Barker 2011). Barker elaborated,

> The success of having these cross-race relationships relies on the presence of same-race connections in the lives of students. These same-race or cultural connections must be embraced and welcomed by the White faculty advisor… Further, Black doctoral students must be strategic and intentional about identifying positive mentors and allies, same-race and cross-race, in addition to their advisor. Such mentors and allies can be supportive and, often times, just listen. (p. 395)

Furthermore, Barker found that faculty advisors believed that it is important for the students to have same-race networks, while their students viewed same-race networks as being critical for their success.

Barker's findings are somewhat different than the results of a study conducted by Patton (2009). Patton studied the mentoring experiences of African American women in graduate and professional schools and found that the participants had mixed feelings about having White mentors. One participant explained that while she felt comfortable asking her mentor general questions, she did not care to connect with him on a deeper level. Patton also shared that a pervasive concern among the participants was that "White mentors were not trustworthy and were unable to and in some cases unwilling to understand their perspectives as African American women" (p. 526). Patton advised that African American women serve as mentors and work to create a network to provide positions and opportunities for African American women in academia.

Zachary (2000) advised that four elements are present in effective cross-cultural mentoring relationships: "a mentor's cross-cultural competency, a flexible cultural lens, well-honed communication skills, and an authentic desire to understand how culture affects the individuals engaged in this relationship" (p. 40). Jiang, a graduate student from China, explained that her culture is very different from the culture in the United States and therefore she had a lot of mentoring needs when she first arrived in the United States for her graduate studies. She stated that through mentoring, her mentor "had a chance to know a student from a different background in terms of culture, language, and perspectives" (personal communication, 2014). An implication from Barker's (2011) study revealed that faculty advisors need to engage in professional development in order to provide effective cross-cultural advisement.

References

Barker, M. J. (2011). Racial context, currency and connections: Black doctoral student and white advisor perspectives on cross-race advising. *Innovations in Education and Teaching International, 48*(4), 387–400.

Cohen, N. H., & Galbraith, M. W. (1995). Mentoring in the learning society. In M. W. Galbraith & N. H. Cohen (Eds.), *Mentoring: New strategies and challenges* (pp. 5–14). San Francisco, CA: Jossey-Bass.

Collins, T., Slough, S., & Waxman, H. (2009). Lessons learned about mentoring junior faculty in higher education. *Academic Leadership, 7*(2), 18–22.

Daloz, L. A. (1999). *Mentor: Guiding the journey of adult learners*. San Francisco, CA: Jossey-Bass.

Evans, K. M., & Packer-Williams, C. L. (2011). Retaining and reclaiming ourselves: Reflections on a peer mentoring group experience for new African American women professors. *Perspectives in Peer Programs, 23*(1), 9–23.

Johnson, W. B. (2007). *On being a mentor: A guide for higher education faculty*. Mahwah, NJ: Lawrence Erlbaum Associates.

Lea, Y. (2011). On mentoring: When the student is ready, the teacher will appear. *International Journal of Learning, 18*(1), 259–268.

Lechuga, V. M. (2011). Faculty-graduate student mentoring relationships: Mentors' perceived roles and responsibilities. *Higher Education, 62*(6), 757–771.

Mansson, D. H., & Myers, S. A. (2012). Using mentoring enactment theory to explore the doctoral student-advisor mentoring relationship. *Communication Education, 61*(4), 309–334.

Miller, M. T., & Deggs, D. (2012). The changing paradigm of graduate student professional socialization and mentoring in graduate adult education programs. *Journal of Faculty Development, 26*(2), 24–28.

Miller, M. T., & Dirkx, J. M. (1995). Mentoring in graduate education: The role of graduate student organizations. *Journal of Adult Education, 23*(1), 20–30.

Nakamura, J., Shernoff, D. J., & Hooker, C. H. (2009). *Good mentoring: Fostering excellent practice in higher education*. San Francisco, CA: Jossey-Bass.

Patton, L. D. (2009). My sister's keeper: A qualitative examination of mentoring experiences among African American women in graduate and professional schools. *Journal of Higher Education, 80*(5), 510–537.

Zachary, L. J. (2000). *The mentor's guide: Facilitating effective learning relationships*. San Francisco, CA: Jossey-Bass.

Chapter 5
Mentoring Undergraduate Students

Abstract There are many opportunities for faculty to mentor undergraduate students in higher education. This chapter begins with an overview of mentoring undergraduate students before turning toward one of the most important ways in which mentoring occurs, undergraduate advisement. Student advisement is a critical aspect of the faculty member's role. Consideration for the needs of non-traditional students is also addressed. Another opportunity for mentoring undergraduate students is found in coursework and projects. This chapter highlights examples of mentoring associated with coursework, along with creative teaching strategies that extend learning. These strategies include lesson study; expert residencies, such as a grant-funded artist residency; interdisciplinary collaborations, such as Wild about Books; and scholarly projects. The chapter concludes with a discussion on mentoring women and students from minoritized racial and ethnic groups.

Keywords Mentoring · Mentoring undergraduates · Lesson study · Artist residencies · Mentoring female undergraduates · Mentoring undergraduates from minoritized racial and ethnic groups

5.1 Introduction

Mentoring opportunities abound in the college classroom. The professor has a direct impact on sparking the students' desire to learn and extend learning into students' future professions and daily lives. Johnson (2007) noted that when college freshmen "are actively engaged by faculty, they are more likely to return for the sophomore year and are more likely thereafter to persist until graduation" (p. 7). One example of faculty actively engaging students is shown by an assistant departmental chairperson who mentors undergraduate students by helping them with their schedules, assisting them with problems, etc. (Paquette, personal communication, 2014).

Mentors generally have a wider role than the traditional faculty advisor because of their individualized approach to instruction (Daloz 1999). The mentor must

D.M. Laverick, *Mentoring Processes in Higher Education*,
SpringerBriefs in Education, DOI 10.1007/978-3-319-39217-2_5

develop a rapport with the protégé and build trust. If not, the protégé will not seek the mentor out for advice and support (Deyarmin, personal communication, 2014). Further, Deyarmin explained that mentoring helps students work through situations that may be difficult or new to them. According to Nientimp, "Oftentimes students enter college with little information about what to actually do other than just show up. Mentors can help guide students and encourage them to make good choices" (personal communication, 2014). Furthermore, they have someone they can trust to give them advice or point them down the right path. Ford has an open-door policy with her advisees (pseudonym, personal communication, 2014). She explained that she listens to personal challenges and helps students get professional help when needed. Daloz (1999) shared that mentors may establish trust by mirroring the language and movements of their students. This advice is especially important when helping advisees who are working through difficult situations.

A personalized approach to mentoring shows protégés that they are valued. This personalized approach to mentoring is evident in the way that a faculty mentor builds relationships and supports her protégés. She explained:

> I establish that I am a listening ear, I am confidential, I am caring and I am willing to assist in any way that I can... Sometimes they need a ride to take the MCAT, LSAT or some other internship or appointment. I know my limits and seek support from others that have the expertise that they need. (Johnson, personal communication, 2014)

Faculty mentors can help undergraduates be successful, which in turn helps with retention. Additionally, faculty can serve as role models for life-long learning (Ford, pseudonym, personal communication, 2014). A specific example that relates to helping undergraduate students become successful is seen in the way that a mentor provided support and mentorship when she "adopted" one student as her own after the loss of the student's mother and stepfather (Infinity, pseudonym, personal communication, 2014). This faculty member provided the student with educational, professional, and personal support on a weekly (and sometimes daily) basis. From a student perspective, mentoring is important "because it prepares students in college for the new chapters of their lives that they are about to begin in the 'real world'" (Carney, personal communication, 2014). Daloz (1999) explained that mentors help shape students' vision of themselves that "is based on their own experience rather than images they have absorbed from others" (p. 148).

5.2 Mentoring Through Advisement

There are components to the advisement process that are procedural but these procedures should not dominate the faculty-student relationship. Advisement presents an opportunity to mentor students and support them in finding success in higher education. Johnson (2007), citing the work of Schlosser et al. (2003), distinguished between advisement and mentoring by stating that "mentoring nearly always refers to a positive relationship focused on the faculty member's strong commitment to the protégé's development and success," while "advising refers to a relationship that may be positive, negative, or insignificant and that may or may not include guidance and skill development" (p. 23).

Mentorship is crucial for new students and as students advance, the relationship provides additional mentoring opportunities as advisees approach commencement and begin searching for a job. The expertise of the advisor should go beyond helping students to schedule classes and teach them about their field of study. Advisors are in a unique position to share with their advisees the opportunities that abound in their field. Their mentorship can open doors for their advisees as they pursue graduate study or begin their career.

The transition to college can be difficult for some students. It is likely that it is the first time that they have stayed away from home for a great length of time. The role of the advisor, as a mentor, is so important in this respect. As one student shared, the mentor is someone students feel comfortable to go to when they have questions and problems; mentoring provides a support system while students are at college and away from their families (Deyarmin, personal communication, 2014). Another student explained, "With all the rules, regulations, and requirements, it is very important to have people that understand the complicated system. It is comforting to know that someone is there to help" (Malicky, personal communication, 2014). Furthermore, because undergraduate students need support and may be unaware of their options, mentoring can share these options with the students (Bono, personal communication, 2014).

Helterbran recommended that advisors care about advising and view advisement as the heart of good teaching, rather than an add-on (personal communication, 2014). Further, she noted that faculty should seek ways to support and encourage students and treat students as they would want to have their own children (or oneself) treated. Students are perceptive about the level of care shown by the advisor. To develop a rapport, one student recommended that advisors begin by asking questions to build a rapport (Deyarmin, personal communication, 2014). Taking time to ask advisees questions helps mentors get to know their protégés on a personal level and therefore builds strong relationships. Daloz (1999) explained that the mentoring relationship feels special. He elaborated, "The student feels uniquely *seen* by the mentor, and if the mentor is endowed with particularly desirable qualities of unusual power in the world, the effect can be a potent tonic" (p. 214). With this advice in mind, the first impression that mentors make on an advisee is crucial in forging a positive relationship in which the advisor eventually is viewed as more than advisor and takes on the role of mentor.

As one example of an individualized approach to mentoring during advisement, students who transfer may encounter unique challenges to scheduling courses. For example, when the course sequence calls for a linear progression of courses that have prerequisites, registering for courses can be difficult. The role of the mentor becomes one of helping students get the courses that they need in order to finish the program (Helterbran, personal communication, 2014). Another example of taking on an individualized approach to advisement is through helping students "find clubs or organizations that will enhance their professional and personal growth" (Infiniti, pseudonym, personal communication, 2014). Furthermore, Infiniti has convinced students to overcome challenges and finish their education in times of personal and professional struggles.

One student shared that it is important that advisors be available as much as possible and establish that they are there to help and talk when needed (Deyarmin, personal communication, 2014). She explained that when they aren't able to meet face-to-face, they need to answer e-mails in a timely fashion and/or hold phone conferences. When mentors make time to effectively mentor undergraduate students, they are demonstrating care and concern; doing so is critical in building positive mentoring relationships.

A mentoring program at North Carolina A&T State was described by Kurepa (2012) who explained that finding time to advise and mentor students can be problematic. Kurepa detailed the Mathematics Learning Community at this institution in which up to 30 math majors may participate. This program, according to Kurepa, requires the students to engage in research projects and enrichment activities as they receive vertical peer mentoring, tutoring, and advising. Kurepa explained that the students in the group have three additional faculty advisors who assist them. Furthermore, the students must also conduct mentoring themselves. Vertical peer mentoring, according to Kurepa, refers to the students mentoring each other. The benefits of Kurepa's approach include the experience that upperclassmen share with freshmen and sophomores, along with the tutoring opportunity that their advanced knowledge of the field provides. Kurepa studied this program and found that the majority of the participants believed they had a strong sense of belonging; many planned to go to graduate school and were confident in their ability to mentor others. Furthermore, Kurepa concluded that the students were more involved in their major, demonstrated commitment to their field, and showed an understanding of being responsible for their careers. From the students' perspective, Kurepa shared that the students were more satisfied with their advising experiences because they had multiple advisors. The faculty advisors, according to Kurepa, also felt greater satisfaction with advisement.

5.2.1 Mentoring Nontraditional Students

A model for mentoring adult learners at State University of New York, Empire State College, was shared by DeSouza (2014). DeSouza explained that mentors go beyond the typical role of the advisor by often being the first point of contact from enrollment through graduation in this highly individualized early childhood care and education program. She elaborated by sharing how these mentors are resources who act as motivators, facilitators, and consultants as they help the adult learners meet challenges that relate to work, family, and college. DeSouza recommended that adult learners be supported through a mentoring model that pairs students with faculty who are accessible and who provide support and encouragement.

Accessibility was also found by Thurston et al. (2009) to be important to protégés. Thurston et al.'s research suggested the following ideas for promoting regular contact with protégés: dropping in, calling, sending e-mail, and having lunch.

5.3 Mentoring Through Coursework and Related Projects

The following section describes ways in which university faculty, primarily teacher educators, have provided mentoring through coursework and related projects that extend learning beyond typical assignments. The instructional strategies that relate to teaching preservice teachers could spark ideas for adaptation to other fields in higher education.

5.3.1 Lesson Study

Japanese Lesson Study (see Chap. 4) is a technique that facilitates mentoring relationships. According to Burghes and Robinson (2009), its use has resulted in improved instruction in math and science in Japan. Burghes and Robinson stated that it:

> Is a process in which teachers jointly plan, observe, analyse, and refine actual classroom lessons, called 'research lessons'. It is a widespread initiative in Japan, and an integral part of their preservice teacher training programmes. In addition, lesson study forms the basis of continuing professional development for teachers within their own school and sometimes across schools within a district. (p. 7)

This approach, therefore, would lend itself to mentoring situations because of the opportunities that it provides with regard to collaboration to improve instruction. Given its use with preservice teachers in Japan, as mentioned by Burghes and Robinson, its use could be extended to other disciplines in higher education. Burghes and Robinson listed the following underlying principles of lesson study:

- Teachers learn best from and improve their practice by seeing other teachers teach;
- Teachers who have developed deep understanding of and skill in subject matter pedagogy should share their knowledge and experience with colleagues;
- Teachers should cultivate students' interest and focus on the quality of their learning. (pp. 7–8)

Molina (2012) studied the use of a Microteaching Lesson Study (MLS) and mentor interaction structures with preservice teachers. Molina's doctoral dissertation described Japanese Lesson Study as a strategy that was modified for use with preservice teachers. She used the adapted approach, Microteaching Lesson Study (MLS), which is credited to the work of Fernandez (2005). Fernandez explained:

> MLS can be used in teacher preparation programs to liven courses typically taught through lecture and recitation... As with Japanese lesson study for practicing teachers, MLS engages prospective teachers in a collaborative and recursive process of lesson development, implementation, analysis, and revisions. (p. 209)

Molina (2012) described how the preservice teachers planned, taught, and videotaped their lessons before peer groups analyzed the videos and the instructor's feedback, and revised the lessons. With regard to mentoring, Molina found that "the MLS mentor is a key component in establishing richer and more reflective discourse during the debriefing sessions" (p. 123). Molina found that the participants valued receiving formative feedback by the MLS mentor, rather than summative feedback. Finally, Molina concluded that the participants who had a MLS mentor "grew more in their understanding of pedagogical content knowledge, tended to resolve group issues with mathematics, pedagogy, and collaboration earlier, and valued the experiences more" (p. 129) than the participants who did not have the same interaction structure. Therefore, according to Molina, "The formative feedback and presence of the MLS mentor during the first two debriefing sessions was an important factor in the development of the mathematical teacher knowledge of the elementary preservice teachers who participated" (p. 129) in the study.

5.3.2 Expert Residencies

Expert residencies, such as hosting an artist in residence, provide opportunities for mentoring. The concept of expert residencies refers to having practicing experts in the field participate in a course as a guest instructor. The resident expert has the potential to serve in a mentoring role for students. Residencies allow students the opportunity to make a connection from theory to practice by exposing them to experts to practice in their intended field on a daily basis. Furthermore, when students have experts in residence who become mentors, doors are opened for building human and social capital. Students have a connection to someone in the field who can help them gain access to internships and positions in the field upon graduation.

The author and her colleague, Dr. Joann Migyanka, hosted artist residencies in their co-taught course, Creative Experiences and Play for All PreK to Grade 4 Learners at Indiana University of Pennsylvania. In an artist residency, an artist attends class sessions as a guest instructor and models his or her craft. Artist residencies provide an opportunity for the art professional to foster deep content knowledge by sharing his or her expertise. The students create their own art project based on the instruction provided by the artist. The opportunity for mentoring in an artist residency is found in the relationship that is developed between the students and the artist as the artist provides support and guidance throughout the process of creating art. The author observed the positive interactions with students and the artist as the artist encouraged them to take risks and dispelled some students' notions of their perceived inadequacy as artists. Many students also had the opportunity to apply their newly learned techniques in their field experiences and in turn became the mentors for their elementary school students (Laverick and Migyanka 2014).

5.3.3 Interdisciplinary Collaboration

Faculty from different disciplines may work collaboratively to mentor undergraduate students. The Wild about Books program is an example of how an education librarian mentored preservice teachers in the College of Education-Educational Technology at Indiana University of Pennsylvania (IUP). Heider described her role as a mentor in this program:

> I supervised students in a service-learning program I created called *Wild about Books. Wild about Books,* a collaborative program between Indiana University of Pennsylvania Libraries, IUP's Department of Professional Studies in Education, and IndiKids, the on-campus childcare center at IUP, gives early childhood and elementary education students the chance to practice their read-aloud and teaching skills in a preschool environment. Every Friday at 10AM, three- and four-year-old IndiKids students come to the Children's Reading Room at IUP's Stapleton Library to hear stories read by College of Education student volunteers. After listening to the stories, the preschool children participate in learning activities designed by teacher education students, with the help and guidance of both me and Professional Studies faculty. (personal communication, 2014)

This example describes a partnership between the course instructor and the educational librarian in which students apply the knowledge that they gained in the classroom to an experience in which they actually teach children under the guidance of the librarian. Figure 5.1 shows Dr. Kelly Heider as she mentored Cassie Fay through the Wild about Books program. The educational librarian stated that she serves as a mentor for the students who choose to pursue this enriching learning activity in the following ways:

- Helped preservice teachers develop a career vision and goals;
- connected them with other professionals who could develop their skills or provide them with opportunities in their field;

Fig. 5.1 Dr. Kelly Heider mentoring Cassie Fay during Wild about Books. *Photo credit* Courtney Connell

- helped them learn to teach well by observing their lessons and providing feedback;
- and let them know that I was in the same place they were twenty years ago and know what it's like to be a student teacher.

5.3.4 Scholarly Projects

Faculty mentors who support students in scholarly projects provide them with a wealth of valuable skills. Sibert shared that she collaborated with a student on a technology presentation, along with collaborating with a former student on a national conference presentation for future teachers (personal communication, 2014). Situations in which mentors collaborate with their protégés to fulfill a common goal align with the work of Daloz (1999), who described mentors and protégés as being drawn together to fill a need in each other. While the need may relate to scholarly projects, other needs may also be fulfilled. For example, the intrinsic rewards that are received from the support and guidance that mentors provide their protégés.

One example of how this collaboration was supported by mentoring is shown in Indiana University of Pennsylvania's annual Undergraduate Scholars Forum. The participating students were mentored by a faculty member as they conducted and presented a research study at a forum held at their university. This presentation was subsequently given at an international conference. Through the faculty member's mentoring skills, the students were able to engage in a scholarly project that provided a deeply meaningful experience that went well beyond their coursework and required projects. Furthermore, the faculty member provided support to the students by first immersing them in an opportunity to present at a local venue before taking their presentation to a large-scale professional conference. Figure 5.2 shows undergraduate students and their faculty mentor at the Undergraduate Scholars Forum.

Fig. 5.2 Dr. Ali Kappel and the undergraduate students she mentored for Indiana University of Pennsylvania's Undergraduate Scholars Forum. The students are (from *left* to *right*): William VanEmburg, Michael Pampena, Ashley Rush, Kaitlyn Colbert, and Alexis Potts. *Photo credit* Tenesha Ali

5.4 Mentoring Undergraduate Students that Include Women and Minoritized Racial and Ethnic Groups

Female undergraduate students or those who are from minoritized racial and ethnic groups have unique needs that may be met through mentoring. This section will discuss first the mentoring needs of female undergraduate students before turning toward the needs of those from minoritized racial and ethnic groups.

5.4.1 Mentoring Undergraduate Students Who Are Women

Female undergraduate students have unique mentoring needs, especially as the needs relate to particular majors. According to one former undergraduate, gender-based mentoring is stronger in the field of elementary education because teachers at this level are predominantly female (Malicky, personal communication, 2014). Malicky further explained that while females have many role models and examples at this level, men may have different mentoring needs. An undergraduate who is a senior expressed that she believes that women need a little more emotional support than men when it comes to choosing classes and adjusting to college (Deyarmin, personal communication, 2014). She also shared that in her experience women tend to stress about academics and may need a little extra guidance or encouragement. Similarly, Nientimp observed in her four years of college that "women often tend to plan ahead, worry, and get worked up. Talking to a mentor is something that can [help them become] calm and refocus so they are not so anxious" (personal communication, 2014).

The notion that women have unique mentoring needs was echoed by a faculty member who offered the following perspective:

> Women have unique mentoring needs based on the discipline. Some disciplines are more receptive and supportive of women in higher education. Education is very supportive and receptive. As a mentor of students in other disciplines, some conversations I have had with students is how to navigate the 'invisible' status in class, group projects, and how to make sure that their 'voice' is heard. (Conrad, pseudonym, personal communication, 2014)

5.4.2 Mentoring Undergraduate Students from Minoritized Racial and Ethnic Groups

Diversity means different things to different groups (Scisney-Matlock and Matlock 2001). Scisney-Matlock and Matlock explained,

> Diversity may be perceived only in terms of race and ethnicity while someone else may see it from the perspective of race, gender, geography, sexual orientation, or religion. This is compounded by the fact that diversity or multiculturalism in the classroom generally is defined globally while it can be very specific when dealing with student populations. (p. 77)

Scisney-Matlock and Matlock identified stereotypes that faculty often bring to the mentoring relationship as a barrier. They shared that it is the responsibility of faculty to mentor students of color, regardless of race or ethnicity. Further, they recommended that mentors guide students toward supportive campus resources before problems start. They deemed it essential that students develop multiple and varied relationships.

Second language learners or students who study abroad may face language-related challenges. Faculty should mentor these students by identifying their needs and sharing resources that will support them. One student cautioned that students in this situation may need some aspects of college explained to them; it shouldn't be assumed that they already know information just because the majority of students are aware (Deyarmin, personal communication, 2014). One example, she explained, would be that they might need help in deciphering forms or navigating websites.

References

Burghes, D., & Robinson, D. (2009). Lesson study: Enhancing mathematics teaching and learning. Reading, Berkshire, United Kingdom: CfBT Education Trust. Retrieved from http://www.cimt.plymouth.ac.uk/papers/lessonstudy.pdf

Daloz, L. A. (1999). *Mentor: Guiding the journey of adult learners*. San Francisco, CA: Jossey-Bass.

DeSouza, D. (2014). Educating the early childhood educator. *Young Children, 69*(2), 88–93.

Fernandez, M. L. (2005). Learning through microteaching study in teacher preparation. *Action in Teacher Education, 26*(4), 36–47.

Johnson, W. B. (2007). *On being a mentor: A guide for higher education faculty*. Mahwah, NJ: Lawrence Erlbaum Associates.

Kurepa, A. (2012). Vertical peer mentoring and advising: A structure for student involvement in multi-level advising. *Mentor: An Academic Advising Journal*. Retrieved from https://dus.psu.edu/mentor/2012/04/vertical-peer-mentoring-advising/

Laverick, D. M., & Migyanka, J. M. (2014). Artist residencies: Supporting childhood prestudent teachers' knowledge and pedagogy to promote arts-based learning. *Teaching Artist Journal, 12* (3), 168–176.

Molina, R. (2012). Microteaching lesson study: Mentor interaction structure and its relation to elementary preservice mathematics teacher knowledge development. *FIU Electronic Theses and Dissertations*. Paper 616. Retrieved from http://digitalcommons.fiu.edu/etd/616

Schlosser, L. Z., Knox, S., Moskovitz, A. R., & Hill, C. E. (2003). A qualitative study of the graduate advising relationship: The advisee perspective. *Journal of Counseling Psychology, 50*, 178–188.

Scisney-Matlock, M., & Matlock, J. (2001). Promoting understanding of diversity through mentoring undergraduate students. In A. G. Reinarz & E. R. White (Eds.), *Beyond teaching to mentoring* (pp. 75–84). San Francisco, CA: Jossey-Bass.

Thurston, L. P., Navarrete, L., & Miller, T. (2009). A ten-year faculty mentoring program: Administrator, mentor, and mentee perspectives. *The International Journal of Learning, 16*(4), 401–415.

Chapter 6
Mentoring Opportunities Outside of Academic Buildings: Field Experiences, Student Organizations, and Athletics

Abstract This chapter describes the mentoring opportunities that are possible outside of academic buildings. Specifically, this chapter begins by sharing information about ways in which mentoring occurs through field experiences, through relationships that are developed with undergraduates' site supervisors (i.e., cooperating teachers) and university supervisors who, together, engage in varied and multiple types of mentoring processes. The chapter then turns toward the rich opportunities for mentoring that occur in living-learning communities. Living-learning communities are organized so that learning is not confined strictly to the university classroom but rather is supported and encouraged in residence halls. Faculty members play an important role in living-learning communities as they act as liaisons between the students and their academic departments and colleges. This collaborative approach is situated close to where the students live and brings mentoring opportunities to them. The chapter concludes with a discussion on the role of mentoring in student organizations and athletics, highlighting examples of the such and describing the benefits of mentoring as perceived by students and faculty. Mentoring in these areas occur in relationships built among the students, faculty, coaches, and other professional colleagues.

Keywords Mentoring · Field experiences · Mentoring in student organizations · Living-learning communities · Mentoring in athletics

6.1 Introduction

This chapter describes the mentoring relationships that take place in higher education in settings outside the classroom. While many of these types of relationships involve faculty or coaches, these types of mentoring experiences may stem from field experiences or internships, in living-learning communities, or in student organizations and athletics. Mentoring in these areas helps students thrive outside of the college classroom, allows them to excel in areas beyond academics, and promotes lifelong benefits. This mentorship cycle promotes healthy and positive

D.M. Laverick, *Mentoring Processes in Higher Education*,
SpringerBriefs in Education, DOI 10.1007/978-3-319-39217-2_6

organizations for all who are involved. Faculty advisors and coaches play a large part in leading their organizations and teams and have the added opportunity to be a mentor. A student-athlete who was mentored and who also acted as a mentor suggested that positive mentoring relationships can be developed through becoming involved on campus, playing a sport, joining a club, joining a fraternity or sorority, and joining an honor society (Carney, personal communication, 2014). Daloz (1999) noted that the quality and power of a mentoring relationship should define the mentor rather than an age. As such, the mentoring experiences of students mentoring other students will be described in this chapter, along with faculty and coaches' mentoring relationships outside the classroom.

6.2 Field Experiences and Internships

Students who are involved in field experiences and internships learn valuable on-the-job skills and gain knowledge in an embedded experience that is intended to apply their content knowledge and promote their professional growth. In many cases, site supervisors learn from the intern as well, which indicates that mutual benefits are shared. Further, university faculty who supervise in internship settings bring knowledge and expertise to the partnership that is created. Faculty also have the opportunity to learn from site supervisors and students who are involved in internships, as they become immersed in real-life applications where theory is applied in real-world contexts. Strong mentor-protégé relationships serve to support all of these stakeholders and each one brings skills, knowledge, and dispositions to the relationships that take place among them. As such, each one has much to offer and also learn. This concept is illuminated in professional development schools (PDSs), which provide a model for mentoring processes as the stakeholders engage in collaborative experiences to enhance professional growth. Mentoring through field experiences that take place in PDSs will be shared after the description of mentoring in field experiences in general.

Strong mentoring relationships may be built through field experiences and internships. In fact, "accredited teacher preparation programs will need to reconsider how to establish physical and temporal proximity among methods courses, clinical experiences, and site-based mentoring" (Shuster 2014, p. 173). One way to accomplish this goal, according to Shuster, is to encourage teacher candidates and their mentor teachers to discuss topics that the candidates learned in their coursework and draw connections to what these topics look like in the mentor teachers' practice. From the perspective of a faculty member who has supervised pre-student teachers and student teachers, the job of a mentor is to "assist them in becoming high quality educators whose main goal is to serve children and families" (Infiniti, pseudonym, personal communication, 2014).

Opportunities for mentoring in the field abound. The university supervisor, cooperating teacher (or field supervisor), and peers may act as mentors. McMahon and Piro (2013) conducted a study of preservice teachers' experience with mentoring in a cohort approach to their placement. These researchers found that the mentoring relationship strengthened the participants' professional growth and understanding of professional responsibilities and expectations. They stated, "Rich mentoring experiences within the field experience are required" (McMahon and Piro 2013, p. 19).

The next sections will discuss mentoring during field experiences by university supervisors, cooperating teachers, and peers. While these topics are tailored toward teacher education and the field experiences of preservice teachers, the concepts are applicable to internships and field experiences in other disciplines.

6.2.1 Mentoring by the University Supervisor

Mentoring by a university supervisor occurs through the observations, evaluations, and constructive feedback that a supervisor provides (Malicky, personal communication, 2014). A former student teacher, who has recently graduated, explained that her supervisor supported her when she needed it by answering questions via e-mail and making herself available (Nientimp, personal communication, 2014). This level of availability is important when students are not attending classes on campus. The supervisor needs to be accessible to be an effective mentor.

Having a personal relationship can be a very important part of the mentoring situation because the lessons that are taken away in this type of situation are lessons of life. When a mentoring relationship has a personal component, trust is built and the mentor's role is broadened. One mentor of undergraduate students shared, "Sometimes my undergrads just need to know that they can call me if they need me, some need a home environment experience, some attend church with me, and sometimes they need to chat over a beverage or meal" (Johnson, personal communication, 2014).

One of the mentoring needs for students who are close to graduation relates to questions about employment (Sibert, personal communication, 2014). Having a mentor who is experienced in the field provides the protégé with authentic advice from someone with experience. This experience is valuable to share, as Sibert did through her advisement and through panel presentations. A student shared that mentoring helps students make connections with people who may be in higher positions (Deyarmin, personal communication, 2014). These connections are helpful when students are pursuing employment after graduation.

6.2.2 Mentoring by the Cooperating Teacher

Cooperating teachers, also referred to as mentor teachers, are in a prime position to support student teachers through mentoring. In terms of the way that Nientimp's cooperating teacher mentored her, she shared that her cooperating teacher provided support through materials, resources, and her professional and personal knowledge (personal communication, 2014). This experience was similar to what Malicky experienced, "My cooperating teachers helped me by giving me real-life examples and 'tricks and tips' for effective teaching. They allowed me to do trial and error lessons where they provided feedback and correction" (personal communication, 2014). In some instances, alumni serve as the cooperating teachers for current teacher candidates and this situation is ideal for mentoring. Alumni who have graduated from the same teacher preparation programs as their protégés have a special insight into the expectations of the program and a unique insight into helping their protégés achieve success.

Sayeski and Paulen (2012) examined student teachers' evaluations of their cooperating teachers to determine what practices the student teachers identified as having a positive impact on their professional development. These authors stated that the valuable practices used by cooperating teachers who create quality student teaching experiences may be used for professional development that enhances the mentoring skills of cooperating teachers. The findings of Sayeski and Paulen's study revealed six categories of practices that student teachers found desirable in cooperating teachers: (a) engaging in advance planning; (b) sharing resources; (c) providing constructive and specific feedback; (d) giving multi-modal feedback; (e) modeling effective practices; and (f) demonstrating trust and confidence. With regard to mentoring, Sayeski and Paulsen stated that a frequently expressed sentiment was, "Not all good teachers make good mentors" and suggested that it should actually be stated as, "Only good teachers make good mentors" (p. 127) because those cooperating teachers who contributed value to their student teachers' development "modeled what they preached" (p. 127). Hobson et al. (2012) concurred by stating that they "believe that mentoring can occur with student teachers in schools, however, just because a student teacher is assigned a cooperating teacher does not mean the preservice teacher will be mentored" (p. 68).

Hobson et al.'s (2012) study was guided by Mertz's (2004) Hierarchy of Mentoring Intent and Involvement Levels Framework to determine the impact of mentoring on student teachers. Mertz presented a conceptual model of mentoring and stated that its purpose was to distinguish mentoring from other types of supportive relationships. Mertz's framework illustrated the supportive mentoring relationships "in terms of the primary intent of the relationship and the degree of involvement (intensity) required to realize the intent" (p. 550). The roles are:

> … visualized in a pyramid to reflect the increasing involvement and intensity required by the relationship and the change in primary intent as one moves from the base (modeling) to apex (brokering). The roles are arranged to suggest a hierarchy based on the degree of involvement required by the relationship. The levels are as follows, from the lowest level of involvement (1) to the highest level of involvement (6):
>
> 1. "Role Model, Peer Pal, or Supporter;
> 2. Teacher or Coach;
> 3. Counselor, Advisor, or Guide;
> 4. Sponsor or Benefactor;
> 5. Patron or Protector
> 6. Mentor" (p. 550)

Furthermore, as the roles and involvement (levels) increase, so does the intent, which moves from the lowest level of Psychosocial Development (Modeling) to Professional Development (Advising) to the highest level of Career Advancement (Brokering). Hobson et al. found that the student teachers in their study perceived all six levels of mentoring as being very important for preservice teachers. The results showed that the three highest of the six levels to be (in order from the highest to lowest of these three levels): Level 1-Role Model, Peer Pal, or Supporter; Level 2-Teacher or Coach; and Level 6-Mentor. Hobson et al. also found that the student teachers perceived poor mentors and lack of mentoring to be some of the obstacles to the success of preservice and novice teachers. The participants in this study shared what they believed to be the components needed in mentoring programs for student teachers: "a focus on certification examination preparation, strategies on working with k-12 students of different backgrounds, and assessment of learners. Attention should be given to the preparation and selection of mentors as well" (p. 79).

Ballinger and Bishop (2011) described the importance of mentoring in education because of the strength of the accountability movement. Furthermore, these authors stated,

> Even though mentoring may be shared with the university supervisor, it is the on-site teacher who has the greatest opportunity with daily contact to mold the student teacher; therefore this individual will now be referred to as the mentor teacher. (p. 30)

Ballinger and Bishop also explained that mentor teachers must: be good at building a rapport with their new student teachers who may be nervous; demonstrate care in assessing their needs; encourage them when needed yet also give them room to experiment and develop their own style. These authors outlined four tools that mentor teachers use: (1) goal setting; (2) modeling; (3) feedback; and (4) systematic assessment. Finally, Ballinger and Bishop shared reasons that cooperating teachers should become mentor teachers, which include the feeling of renewal or challenge that veteran teachers may experience, along with the connections and relationships that are built with the student teacher and the university supervisor.

A study conducted by Hennissen et al. (2011) examined preservice teachers' perceptions of their mentor teachers' mentoring skills. These researchers found that six types of mentoring skills used by mentor teachers related to providing emotional support, while five other skills related to task assistance. The six skills providing emotional support were identified by the researchers as: "summarising content, showing attentive behaviour, giving positive opinion, showing genuineness, summarising feeling and giving information," while the five mentoring skills related to task assistance are: "asking for concreteness, helping in finding and choosing alternatives, asking for something new, giving advice and giving information" (p. 1056). According to the authors, the mentoring skills that were identified could be used in professional development programs for improving mentor teachers' mentoring skills.

There are specific tips for mentoring student teachers that university supervisors may communicate to mentor teachers. Larkin (2013) advised that mentor teachers should do the following:

1. Stay with the student teacher rather than leaving them alone, in order to provide the feedback and support that is needed.
2. Provide a running commentary of the mentor's teaching to explain the lesson that is being modeled.
3. Allow the student teacher to be creative in developing their lessons.
4. Model constructivist teaching.
5. Share teaching knowledge that is topic-specific.
6. Model how to learn the content that is being taught.
7. While planning lessons together, focus on articulating what the student teacher want the students to learn.
8. Build time into the schedule to talk with the student teacher.
9. Connect the student teacher to the larger political context of the school.
10. View student teaching as a learning opportunity rather than a performance.

The tips shared by Larkin provide mentor teachers with concrete suggestions that help in making the student teaching experience positive for the student teacher, mentor teacher, and students.

6.2.3 Peer Mentoring

Peer mentoring was explained by Johnson (2007) as when a "member of one's own year group or more advanced students who lend support offer advice, and provide guidance" (p. 95). Undergraduate upper class students who mentored freshmen enrolled in a learning strategies course explained that the strategies related to attitude, anxiety, and motivation were most successful as a result of a peer mentoring program (Rubin 2008). An example of how peer mentoring took place in a professional development school setting is described in the next section.

6.2.4 Professional Development Schools

Professional development schools (PDSs) "are learning organizations where schools and universities share the common goal of preparing quality teachers through enhancing the professional development of novice and veteran teachers" (Carpenter and Sherretz 2012, p. 89). Because of the extended amount of time that student teachers spend in PDSs with their mentor teachers, efficacy in teaching is increased (Epstein and Willhite 2015). PDSs "allow mentor teachers to become involved in teacher preparation and their own professional development and university professors to keep current and connected with K-12 classroom practice" (Schuster 2014, p. 172).

A PDS arrangement with the author's university and two school districts will now be shared in order to highlight the role that mentoring played in supporting the professional growth of the preservice teachers. This arrangement involved the use of cohorts in the Early Childhood (PreK-Grade 6) (ECP6) major. A new cohort was started each year that included sophomores who attained their first step in the approval process of the teacher certification program. Attaining this approval permitted the students to enroll in a blocked sequence of classes that included their first field experience. This field experience, Pre-Student Teaching I, allowed students to visit early learning centers to conduct observations, teach mini-lessons, and assist the teachers as appropriate. Prior to the fall semester of their senior year, the preservice teachers applied for acceptance into their second professional sequence, which included additional blocked courses and the Pre-Student Teaching II field experience. This field experience was unique in that the students took courses for first 10 weeks of the semester on campus, after making five visits to the field and then after the 10 weeks ended, they spent all day, every day in the field until the end of the semester. For the second semester of their senior year, the students spent half of the semester in an early childhood placement (kindergarten through grade 3) and the other half of the semester in an upper elementary school placement (grades four through six). These two field experiences were in the same school district and most often in the same school. All of the field experiences, beginning with the sophomore year, took place in the community that surrounded the two school districts in which the PDSs were located. The mentoring aspect of this arrangement was that the pre-student teachers were mentored by the student teachers in the PDSs. The senior student teachers mentored the pre-student teachers on site and assisted them in getting acclimated to the school community and professional aspects of making the transition from student to teacher. The cycle of mentoring, therefore, progressed from cohort to cohort in this fashion.

6.2.5 Co-teaching

Co-teaching involves two credentialed professionals who offer joint delivery of instruction to a diverse group of students within a shared classroom space (Friend and Cook 2010). Co-teaching during student teaching has been shown by research to be an effective alternate to the traditional approach to student teaching (Maddas 2014). Within a field experience, co-teaching during student teaching offers an innovative way of preparing new teachers (Diana 2014). Diana explained that co-teaching benefits the cooperating teacher as well as the student teacher, due to the professional development experience that this approach provides. When co-teaching is implemented during student teaching, the mentoring experience may be enhanced due to the shared teaching experience. The conversations and teachable moments that occur before, during, and after a co-taught lesson provide mentors and protégés with opportunities to address concerns, discuss challenges, and celebrate successes. Furthermore, Maddas found that cooperating teachers were able to model effective teaching while co-teaching with their student teachers. Furthermore, results from Maddas' study indicated that co-teaching has the potential to change mentoring in teaching. The participants in this study revealed that co-teaching changed the way that they interacted with their student teachers.

6.3 Living-Learning Communities

Living-learning communities (LLCs) are defined as "residential housing programs that incorporate academically based themes and build community through common learning" (Brower and Inkelas 2010, p. 36). In LLCs, faculty mentors collaborate and support peer mentors, meet with students, offer advisement, answer questions, and provide resources that make the residence halls an extension of university classrooms and offices. This approach to mentoring is a form of outreach that brings resources directly to the students. Brower and Inkelas explained that living-learning communities are often referred to as Living-Learning Programs (LLPs). They identified the following program themes found in LLPs:

> Civic and social leadership, disciplinary, fine and creative arts, general academic, honors, sophomores only, cultural, leisure, political interest, residential college, research, upper division (juniors and seniors only), Reserve Officer Training Corp, first-year transition, umbrella (many themes under one banner, such as foreign-language halls), wellness or health, and women. (p. 39)

At Indiana University of Pennsylvania, the author was involved with the one of the living-learning communities, education, as the faculty liaison. Faculty liaisons from different academic colleges within the university and their related disciplines each served their respective living-learning communities by providing advisement and resources. The structure of the living-learning community allowed for mentoring to occur on different levels because of the relationships that were built. For example, the residence halls utilized community assistants (CAs) who had the potential to support and mentor the residents. The CAs, in turn, were guided by a smaller group of peer mentors. As the faculty liaison, the author worked directly with the peer mentors to offer guidance and support. Each of these relationships had the potential to support mentoring. As a faculty liaison, the author had the ability to share ideas for professional workshops that were identified as needs based on their conversations with CAs and residents. For example, the need for books, resources, and speakers to address the topic of passing teacher certification exams was an identified need that residents expressed. The author recommended a guest speaker to describe what tests were needed, how to register, and recommend study materials. Additionally, test-preparation books were purchased for the living-learning community members to share. The author held office hours in the residence hall in order to become more accessible to the residents. This arrangement allowed for mentoring to take place outside of the academic buildings and among residents, the CAs, peer mentors, and faculty liaison. A trickle-down effect took place as the faculty liaison acted as a mentor and modeled ways in which the peer mentors could interact with the community assistants, which in turn affected the ways in which CAs interacted with residents. A recommendation for faculty liaisons is to hold regularly scheduled, formal meetings, at least on a monthly basis, with peer mentors in order to stay in touch with the residents' needs. Holding office hours in the residence hall facilitates relationship building and provides opportunities for informal mentoring.

Garrett and Zabriskie (2004) studied the impact that student participation in LLPs made on their interaction with faculty. Their findings:

> Suggest that students participating in an LLC are more likely to have interactions with faculty members—both at the formal-academic level and the informal-mentor level—than their peers not involved in living-learning programs. Reasons for this difference might be attributed to the structure of the LLC, which provides for easy access to faculty members. (p. 42)

Furthermore, Garrett and Zabriskie (2004) found that "students who lived in a residence hall with a LLC but chose not to participate were found to have small but significantly higher informal-mentor type interactions with faculty members than students who lived in traditional residence halls without LLCs" (p. 42).

> The study conducted by Brower and Inkelas (2010) found:
>
> Even a one-year LLP experience generated lasting effects on students. Those students who had lived in an LLP during their first year in college had higher levels of academic self-confidence, were more likely to be a mentor for other students, and remained more committed to civic engagement *three years later.* (pp. 41–42)

The authors described the following environmental elements that were positively associated with student outcomes: "studying with peers, holding academic or sociocultural discussions with peers, interacting with faculty members on course-related matters, and students' feelings that their residence hall climate is socially supportive and tolerant" (p. 41). Furthermore, "students' perception of their residence hall climate as academically supportive was positively related to all of the student learning outcomes" (p. 41).

6.4 Student Organizations and Athletics

The positive effects of mentoring in student organizations and athletics are beneficial throughout the students' lives. For example, students learn teamwork, become goal-oriented, utilize leadership skills, and develop positive character traits. As faculty advisors and coaches mentor through their leadership and by their example, the students learn important skills that eventually trickle down to the new students joining the organization, which creates a cyclical effect. Mentors in higher education are most often faculty and sports coaches (Daloz 1999). Thus, the role of the mentor may be seen not only in the classroom but also within student organizations and athletics. Mentors in these areas have a unique opportunity to build lasting relationships based on a foundation of shared interests. Coaches act as mentors both in sports and in life (Nientimp, personal communication, 2014).

6.4.1 Mentoring in Student Organizations

Mentoring is important among the members, officers, and advisors in student organizations. Officers and advisors, in particular, play a crucial role in mentoring new members to insure that the organization runs smoothly from year to year. In anticipation of the transition to new leadership, officers should begin early to mentor incoming officers and teach them how their positions are executed. Not only should they concentrate on procedural aspects of the position but they should also share historical information, provide advice on how to be proactive in addressing potential issues, and explain how the organization works as a whole. The former president of an honor society in education explained how the advisors of her organization mentored her as she took over the presidency after the organization had completed a rough year. Her goal was to make the group more organized. She explained,

> With the help of the advisors, I was able to make the organization run much more smoothly and more enjoyable for everyone. The advisors were able to respond to any questions I had via email and phone quickly and help oversee some of the organization logistics. (Deyarmin, personal communication, 2014)

Another way in which mentoring can take place in student organization is through establishing relationships between "littles" and "bigs." This approach was implemented in Indiana University of Pennsylvania's Beta Gamma Chapter of Kappa Delta Pi, which is the international honor society for education. The members of the organization served as "Bigs" who were paired with the new members, "Littles," as a way of mentoring the new members of the organization. The benefits to this approach were seen not only serving the mission of the organization but also in the students' education-related majors. Having a mentor through this organization allowed the littles to seek advice and support from older students who had more experience in their major. In turn, the "Bigs" had an opportunity to learn mentoring skills that would also serve them well in their future careers in education.

From the organization advisor's perspective, faculty involvement in a student organization is important because as Ford explained, she was able to advise students with issues and helped the program at large solve many of the student, curricular, and programmatic issues (pseudonym, personal communication, 2014). Working with students in organizations allows for a closer relationship with faculty advisors to be established. The trust that is built outside the classroom can be helpful in knowing what students' needs and concerns are and then assisting them to address these issues.

6.4.2 *Mentoring in Athletics*

Mentoring in athletics builds cohesiveness in a team. Mentors may be coaches or teammates and therefore athletes may actually have more than one mentor, depending on the role of the mentor and situation. The importance of a coach who serves as a mentor cannot be underestimated. Figure 6.1 illustrates a coaching situation in which mentoring takes place.

A college softball player shared the following perspective on her experiences in being mentored at the university level:

> I have been mentored by several people at Indiana University of Pennsylvania. For starters, I have been blessed to be a part of such a special softball program at IUP. The upper classmen taught me what it means to be a student-athlete and how to manage my time wisely with my studies and softball schedule. Though it was not always easy, the constant support from my teammates encouraged me to work hard and get the job done, both on and off the field. The College of Education at IUP has some of the best professors in Pennsylvania. I was very fortunate to have professors who actually knew me by name and cared about how I was doing with my studies and life outside of the classroom. They increased my desire to learn and also increased my knowledge in the field of Special Education and Early Childhood Education. My softball team and the professors here at IUP are currently helping me strive to achieve my goal as a future teacher so that I can be a role model for my fellow teammates who are underclassman as well as the students that someday I will teach. (Carney, personal communication, 2014)

While the previous quote illustrated how a student-athlete was mentored, she continued by describing how she transformed into a mentor due to being an upperclassman on her team:

> Last year, as a junior on the softball team I was considered an upper classman. I took my role as an upper classman very seriously. I was a role model and mentor to the underclassman who were freshman and sophomores. It was important to me that I exemplified the importance of what it meant to be a student-athlete at Indiana University of Pennsylvania. Student-athletes are held a higher standard than most students at IUP. In order to be an athlete, we must maintain a certain GPA or we will not be eligible to play sports. Also, it is important that we stay out of trouble and away from anything that may put

Fig. 6.1 College softball recruit, Alaina Laverick, being mentored and coached by her father, Randy Laverick. *Photo credit* William Hamilton

> our sports careers on the line. However, being a student athlete at IUP has many benefits and great experiences. The traveling, staying in hotels, eating out, and getting away from the campus for a few days are always a huge benefit. The memories and the relationships made with teammates and coaches last a lifetime. From experience, after a long day of traveling and playing two softball games three to five times a week or possibly more, can be very exhausting. When I want to go to bed or just relax, I remember I have to study, do homework, write papers, and so on, all of which is very important. Notice how student comes before athlete in student-athlete. When we graduate college and are starting new chapters in our life and pursuing our careers and interviewing for jobs, what we did in softball is not important. What is important is our degree and how we performed and worked in our studies. As a mentor and role model, for me, it is very important that I am able to help the underclassman understand that. As a student-athlete, time management is key to success. (Carney, personal communication, 2014)

This quote is illustrative of the description provided by Lea (2011) who stated that "mentoring creates and results in a lasting transformational impact in the engaged persons" (p. 259). Figure 6.2 depicts the mentoring relationship between a softball player who is an upperclassman and her protégé, an underclassman teammate.

Faculty advisors and coaches play a large part in leading their teams and organizations and have the added opportunity to be a mentor. Dungy (2010) addressed the concept of mentor leaders in his book, *The Mentor Leader: Secrets to Building People and Teams that Win Consistently*. Dungy intimated that he saw

Fig. 6.2 Upperclassman, Meghan Carney, mentoring her teammate, Hannah Mercer, in softball. *Photo credit* Diane McCoy

many leaders in his life but the ones who had the greatest positive impact were those who were also mentors. He stated,

> Success for a mentor leader is measured by different standards than those commonly accepted in our society. Mentor leadership is all about shaping, nurturing, empowering, and growing. It's all about relationships, integrity, and perpetual learning. Success is measured in changed lives, strong character, and eternal values rather than in material gain, temporal achievement, or status. Ultimately, mentor leadership is just as successful in achieving the standards of accomplishment in our society. But unlike other types of leadership, it is primarily concerned with building and adding value to the lives of people in the process. It is about changing lives. (p. xviii)

Dungy's quote puts into perspective the role that coaches and advisors of student organizations play in mentoring university students. He stated, "Mentor leadership focuses on building people up and building leaders for the next generation" (p. 9). In reference to the cyclical effect of mentorship discussed in this chapter, Dungy's perspective is that "mentor leaders produce mentor leaders" (p. 42).

The mentoring relationships that take place in athletics build students who are leaders and who give back by becoming mentors themselves. For student-athletes who have increased demands on their time, having strong and supportive mentors make the difference in their success. These mentors build student-athletes' success in academics, sports, and in life.

References

Ballinger, D. A., & Bishop, J. G. (2011). Mentoring student teachers: Collaboration with physical education teacher education. *Strategies: A Journal for Physical and Sport Education, 24*(4), 30–34.

Brower, A. M., & Inkelas, K. (2010). Living-learning programs: One high-impact educational practice we know a lot about. *Liberal Education, 96*(2), 36–43.

Carpenter, B. D., & Sherretz, C. E. (2012). Professional development school partnerships: An instrument for teacher leadership. *School-University Partnerships, 5*(1), 89–101.

Daloz, L. A. (1999). *Mentor: Guiding the journey of adult learners*. San Francisco, CA: Jossey-Bass.

Diana, T. J. (2014). Co-teaching: Enhancing the student teaching experience. *Kappa Delta Pi Record, 50*(2), 76–80.

Dungy, T. (with Whitaker, N.). (2010). *The mentor leader: Secrets to building people and teams that win consistently*. Carol Stream, IL: Tyndale House Publishers.

Epstein, A., & Willhite, G. L. (2015). Teacher efficacy in an early childhood professional development school. *International Electronic Journal of Elementary Education, 7*(2), 189–198.

Friend, M., & Cook, L. (2010). *Interactions: Collaboration skills for school professionals*. Boston: Pearson.

Garrett, M. D., & Zabriskie, M. S. (2004). The influence of living-learning program participation on student-faculty interaction. *Journal of College & University Student Housing, 33*(1), 38–44.

Hennissen, P., Crasborn, F., Brouwer, N., Korthagen, F., & Bergen, T. (2011). Clarifying preservice teacher perceptions of mentor teachers' developing use of mentoring skills. *Teaching and Teacher Education, 27*(6), 1049–1058.

Hobson, L. D., Harris, D., Buckner-Manley, K., & Smith, P. (2012). The importance of mentoring novice and preservice teachers: Findings from a HBCU student teaching program. *Educational Foundations, 26*(3–4), 67–80.
Johnson, W. B. (2007). *On being a mentor: A guide for higher education faculty*. Mahwah, NJ: Lawrence Erlbaum Associates.
Larkin, D. B. (2013). 10 things to know about mentoring student teachers. *Phi Delta Kappan, 94* (7), 38–43.
Lea, Y. (2011). On mentoring: When the student is ready, the teacher will appear. *International Journal of Learning, 18*(1), 259–268.
Maddas, R. M. (2014). *Co-teaching as a teacher preparation model: A qualitative study of cooperating teachers' perceptions*. (Doctoral dissertation). Retrieved from Proquest. (UMI Number 3665897).
McMahon, S., & Piro, J. (2013). Mentoring in a field experience. *Field Experience Journal, 11*, 18–37.
Mertz, N. T. (2004). What's a mentor anyway? *Educational Administration Quarterly, 40*(4), 541–560. doi:10.1177/0013161X04267110
Rubin, J. B. (2008). *The effects of peer mentoring on a college developmental learning strategies classroom*. (Doctoral dissertation). Available from ProQuest Dissertations and Theses database (UMI No. 3307304).
Sayeski, K. L., & Paulsen, K. J. (2012). Student teacher evaluations of cooperating teachers as indices of effective mentoring. *Teacher Education Quarterly, 39*(2), 117–130.
Schuster, D. (2014). Creating more seamless connections between university-based coursework and school-based mentoring. *Kappa Delta Pi Record, 50*(4), 170–174.

MIX
Papier aus verantwortungsvollen Quellen
Paper from responsible sources
FSC® C105338

If you have any concerns about our products,
you can contact us on
ProductSafety@springernature.com

In case Publisher is established outside the EU,
the EU authorized representative is:
Springer Nature Customer Service Center GmbH
Europaplatz 3, 69115 Heidelberg, Germany

Printed by Libri Plureos GmbH
in Hamburg, Germany